The Kilfenora Teaboy

The Kilfenora Teaboy
A Study of Paul Durcan
is first published in 1996
in Ireland by
New Island Books,
2 Brookside,
Dundrum Road,
Dublin 14,
Ireland.

ISBN   1 874597 31 6

New Island Books receives financial assistance from
The Arts Council (An Chomhairle Ealaíon),
Dublin, Ireland.

Cover design by Jon Berkeley
Typeset by Graphic Resources
Printed in Ireland by Colour Books, Ltd.

The Kilfenora Teaboy

A Study of Paul Durcan

Edited by

Colm Tóibín

NEW
ISLAND
BOOKS

The works of Paul Durcan

ENDSVILLE (with Brian Lynch)
New Writers Press, Dublin, 1967

O WESTPORT IN THE LIGHT OF ASIA MINOR
Anna Livia Press, Dublin, 1975. Revised edition (containing poems from *Endsville*), Harvill, London, 1995

TERESA'S BAR
Gallery Press, Dublin, 1976

SAM'S CROSS
Poetry Ireland Press, Dublin, 1978

JESUS, BREAK HIS FALL
Raven Arts Press, Dublin, 1980

ARK OF THE NORTH
Published on the occasion of Francis Stuart's 80th Birthday, by Raven Arts Press, Dublin, 1982

THE SELECTED PAUL DURCAN (edited by Edna Longley)
Blackstaff Press, Belfast, 1982

JUMPING THE TRAIN TRACKS WITH ANGELA
Raven Arts Press, Dublin, 1983

THE BERLIN WALL CAFÉ
Blackstaff Press, Belfast, 1985

GOING HOME TO RUSSIA
Blackstaff Press, Belfast, 1987

IN THE LAND OF PUNT (with Gene Lambert)
Clashganna Mills Press, 1988

JESUS AND ANGELA
Selections from *Jesus, Break His Fall* and *Jumping the Train Tracks with Angela*, Blackstaff Press, Belfast, 1988

DADDY, DADDY
Blackstaff Press, Belfast, 1990

CRAZY ABOUT WOMEN
National Gallery of Ireland, Dublin, 1991

A SNAIL IN MY PRIME (New and Selected Poems)
Harvill, London, 1993

GIVE ME YOUR HAND
National Gallery, London, 1995

Contents

Portrait of the Artist as a Spring Lamb

Colm Tóibín

The people had started to join in; the crowd had begun to respond as he read his poem. Our Lady of Knock, pray for us. Our Lady of Barnalyra, pray for us. Our Lady of Ballavarry, pray for us. Our Lady of Portacloy, pray for us. Our Lady of Carrahully, pray for us. Our Lady of Straide, pray for us. Our Lady of Partry, pray for us. Our Lady of Ballycroy, pray for us. Our Lady of Pontoon, pray for us. Our Lady of Keel, pray for us. Our Lady of Cong, pray for us. Our Lady of Deereenascuba, pray for us. Our Lady of Tournakeady, pray for us. Our Lady of Loughnafooey, pray for us. Our Lady of Barnacuige, pray for us.

On the way to Dublin Airport to catch the flight to Knock they had heard the news and weather forecast on the radio. It had been fine all morning, but it was darkening now, the weather was going to get worse. Mr Haughey seemed relaxed; he waved out at the driver of a car who gave him right of way. No one said anything, but doubt grew in Paul Durcan's mind as to whether they would be able to take off or not.

The pilot and co-pilot, however, were ready in the small plane; Mr Haughey was there with his wife and they were to be accompanied to Knock for the opening of the airport by Brian Lenihan and P J Mara.

Mr Haughey had commissioned Paul Durcan to write a poem for the opening of the airport. He would fly with them.

The plane flew low, incredibly low; the plane was bouncing around in the air. They flew over roof-tops, over Trim, over Longford and then north. They flew over the bogs; they were over Mayo; the rain was pouring down. They could see cattle huddling for shelter. The pilot would not be able to make an instrument landing. Ahead of schedule, they circled over the new airport for a while. At one stage, so bad was the weather that the plane was actually on its side in the air. "Tell the control tower we're coming in," Mr Haughey said to the pilot. The rain had just stopped. As they approached the runway, it looked like a whale's back surfacing.

There were crowds everywhere, the sort of crush you feel in Croke Park when the match is over and you're trying to get out.

Mr Haughey and Monsignor Horan talked for a while. Paul Durcan was introduced to Horan and liked him, thought he looked like a Russian.

The rain was like nothing on earth, it was pouring down. Everyone had to shout because of the noise of the wind and the rain. They waited on the platform. Paul Durcan got a sense there, he can't put it succinctly, but he felt something, something of Ireland a hundred years ago, Ireland during the Famine: the crowd, the rain, the wind, the land all around, the quality of the desolation. The dark edge of the world. He's not sure how to describe it, but he did feel it, and it was overwhelming.

Can you imagine, he asks, trying to read a poem under these circumstances, a poem that you know is ten minutes long? Can you imagine what it is like to wait there in the middle of a storm on the top of a mountain, while Mr Haughey speaks and then cuts the tape, knowing that you have to hold these drenched people with a long poem?

I am Raftery the poet smoking my pipe in Knock airport
Sitting in the arrivals lounge with my legs crossed
Taking off and landing by the light of my heart.

The poem was in sections, full of the mystery, incantation, mockery, irony, pity, humour, naïvety, risk and sorrow which fill Paul Durcan's poems. *Lady of drumlins, picnic with us. Lady of fuchsia, weep for us. Lady of whins, laugh with us. Lady of seaweed, be silent with us. Lady of moorhens, call for us. Lady of salmon, leap for us. Lady of mackerel, school us. Lady of haystacks, save us. Lady of trees, plant us. Lady of deer, rear us. Lady of turf, stack us. Lady of donkeys, fly with us. Lady of sleep, sleep with us. Lady of dragonflies, sparkle with us. Lady of computers, delight us.*

His reading was followed by a harpist. The crowd sang The West's Awake. His poem was accompanied by a series of downpours, but now the rain had eased again. For a second when someone roared up at him: "Paul, you were great", he really believed that it was an aunt of his, an aunt whom he had known in Mayo, he really believed that he saw her in the crowd, he looked down, she'd been dead ten years but for that second he was sure it was her. It was the sort of thing she would shout up.

Mayo has haunted him like that. His parents were both from Mayo. He spent holidays in Mayo with both sides of the family.

The village of Turlough in the heartland of Mayo,
And my father's mother's house, all oil-lamps and
    women,
And my bedroom over the public bar below,
And in the morning cattle cries and cock crows:
Life's seemingly seamless garment gorgeously rent
By their screeches and bellowings. And in the evenings
I walked with my father in the high grass down by the
    river
Talking with him — an unheard-of thing in the city.
        ('Going Home to Mayo, Winter 1949')

There were things in Mayo which couldn't be talked about: the Civil War, certain things about the family. His grandfather was Joseph McBride, brother of John McBride, who was shot by the British after 1916, who had married Maud Gonne. He pestered his granny with questions about John McBride, Maud Gonne, Yeats. He remembers being brought to Roebuck House to see Maud Gonne and running away from her in terror. In old age, she looked like a bird in the bed. Her hands looked like claws.

Dublin was alien, full of terror, hard, masculine. Coming back from Mayo was a nightmare. They lived off Leeson Street. Even still, now, in new poems, the names of places in Ireland have a special hold over him, the litany of names which has also preoccupied Brian Friel.

Kilcock, Kinnegad, Strokestown, Elphin,
Tarmonbarry, Tulsk, Ballaghaderreen, Ballavarry.
        ('Going Home to Mayo, Winter 1949')

There are times in his work when places in Ireland are offered a sort of sanctity and holiness which is given to the towns of the New Testament, or the places invoked in the Psalms.

Back in the town of Cahir,
In the Glen of Aherlow,
Not far from Peekaun
In the townland of Toureen,
At the foot of Galtee Mór
In the County of Tipperary.

('The Haulier's Wife Meets Jesus on the
Road Near Moone')

In the family, the extended family, his being a writer is always attributed to a long illness he suffered when he was thirteen, but he remembers inspiration stirring at an earlier stage. All his life he has been deeply affected, impressed and influenced by people he has come across: Nessa, whom he married, writers like Brian Lynch, Leland Bardwell, Michael Hartnett, Anthony Cronin, Francis Stuart, Patrick Kavanagh, whom he has known. He still talks with reverence about his Jesuit English teacher Joe Veale, who stood apart from the relentless misogyny and relentless imputation of guilt which permeated his education.

Books became a way of dealing with the world: George Orwell's *1984*, Graham Greene's *The Heart of the Matter*, T S Eliot's *Murder in the Cathedral*; poets such as Ezra Pound, Hopkins, Hart Crane, Wallace Stevens, Emily Dickinson, Robert Frost were all magic to him.

He took classes in painting — painting remains an obsession — and acting. Later at UCD he would study theology, as well as the more mundane subjects. All his life sport has been a major interest.

He left UCD in the middle of 1964 without taking a degree and made his way to London. In 1966 as the whole country was celebrating the life and death of McDonogh and

McBride, Connolly and Pearse, he was a full-time resident in London, obsessed with the World Cup and Muhammad Ali, far from the madding crowd at home. Twenty years later, he doesn't want to talk about the family's response to his activities at that time, he hovers over the matter, makes a few remarks and falls silent.

He had trouble finding work in London, eventually joining Securicor in the company of Michael Hartnett, thereafter getting jobs washing dishes and going to work for the North Thames Gas Board at the beginning of 1967 as a clerk for ten pounds a week. It was five minutes walk from the Tate Gallery and he used to spend lunch-time every day looking at the paintings of Francis Bacon. Opposite the entrance to the Gas Board there was a big sign which said: 'Look Ahead With Gas'. Finally, he couldn't stand it any more and came back to Dublin.

He is dubious about the phrase 'turning point', he doesn't like it, and is hesitant about using it to describe what happened to him when he came back to Dublin in the spring of 1967. Years before, when he was still at school, he had heard Joe Veale, his English teacher, talking about Patrick Kavanagh and he had even wandered along to the L&H at UCD to see Kavanagh. He was deeply shocked by the treatment of Kavanagh, by his entrance and presence; Kavanagh seemed to resemble a caged beast.

He now found himself in the company of Patrick Kavanagh and Katharine Kavanagh more or less every day. Kavanagh was wonderful company. At the same time Brian Lynch brought out the book *Endsville* with poems by himself and Paul Durcan. Kavanagh liked *Endsville* and introduced Paul Durcan to his London publisher Timothy O'Keefe, of McGibbon and Kee, who asked him for a manuscript, and wrote a few weeks later saying that he wanted to publish the book the following autumn and that a contract would come soon. The letter burnt a hole in his back pocket.

McGibbon and Kee never published the book because they were taken over by Granada and the editors had to leave. By the time another publisher could be found, the North had blown up and Northern poets were big news; Southern Irish poetry went underground where it has remained, in effect, ever since.

On 1 August 1967 Patrick Kavanagh and Katharine were going to a wedding at the Shangri-La Hotel in Dalkey. Paul Durcan wasn't invited to the wedding but it was arranged that he and Patrick would arrive just as the breakfast was coming to an end. They got a taxi out. It was a lovely sunny day and he said to Patrick that it reminded him of being in Mount Mellory monastery. Patrick told him he shouldn't be thinking about monasteries; it was women he should be thinking about.

The waiters went to throw the two late-comers out, but the best man intervened. Paul Durcan found himself up at the bar, there was a woman beside him, they started talking. He thought that she was beautiful and she asked him if he would like to go for a swim. Her name was Nessa.

I met her on the First of August
In the Shangri-La Hotel,
She took me by the index finger
And dropped me in her well.
And that was a whirlpool, that was a whirlpool,
And I very nearly drowned.

('Nessa')

A week later Nessa went back to London where she was working; he followed her after a few weeks, but had to return to Dublin for an interview for a job as a sports sub-editor at the *Irish Press*. He got the job and was due to start on 4 December.

A week beforehand, he was in a pub with Brian Lynch who told him that Patrick Kavanagh wasn't well, that he had taken a turn. The next morning his mother woke him to tell him that Kavanagh was dead.

I awoke with a pain in my head
And my mother standing at the end of the bed;
"There's bad news in the paper," she said
"Patrick Kavanagh is dead."

('November 1967')

It was a nightmare. He couldn't believe it. On the Saturday the funeral took place in Iniskeen and on the Sunday he was due to start in the *Irish Press* at half-past five. Nessa had come home. Nobody told him to do anything when he went in to the paper, he was left sitting there. He was there until half-past one.

The next day, he said goodbye to Nessa on O'Connell Street Bridge and walked down Burgh Quay, walked past the *Irish Press*, down a side street, into the bar of The Red Bank and about an hour later walked back up. He had been serious about the job, it had taken a lot of organising; by abandoning it, he knew he had sealed his fate.

London was definite now. He went and stayed with Harriet Waugh, who was a friend of Nessa's and waited for her to return to London.

Around the corner from Francis Bacon
Was where we made our first nest together
On the waters of the flood;
Where we first lived in sin:
The sunniest, most virtuous days of our life.

('Around the Corner from Francis Bacon')

They moved to Barcelona, where he found a job teaching at the Casa Ingles and they stayed until Christmas, when they returned to London and got married. Nessa was the bread-winner; Paul Durcan looked after their two children and wrote reviews. There was a problem about going back to Ireland. They both agreed that they didn't want to live in Dublin; they decided to go to Cork where he would do a degree and become a teacher and Nessa would get a teaching qualification. He enrolled in UCC in the autumn of 1971; the children were two and one.

Things were tough, but Cork was wonderful, it felt thousands of miles from Dublin.

At the high window, shipping from all over the world
Being borne up and down the busy, yet contemplative,
    river;
Skylines drifting in and out of skylines in the cloudy
    valley;
Firelight at dusk, and city lights in the high window.

('"Windfall", 8 Parnell Hill, Cork')

He took archaeology as a fourth subject and became inspired by the lectures of Michael J O'Kelly; his lectures were pure poetry from start to finish; Paul Durcan got firsts in everything except English in his first year; he decided to drop English and do a degree in archaeology and medieval history. It brought him back to the world of place names, to the magic nature of rural Ireland; it brought him back to the golden world of Mayo. M J O'Kelly was giving him back his own country; it was magic, absolute magic.

*My vocabularies are boulders cast up on time's
    beaches;*
Masses of sea-rolled stones reared up in mile-high ricks
Along the shores and curving coast of all my island;
Verbs dripping fresh from geologic epochs;
Scorched, drenched, in metamorphosis, vulcanicity,
    ice ages.

('Before the Celtic Yoke')

To get a job he would have to do an MA. Nessa had trained as a remedial teacher. A couple of weeks after the final exam, while he was thinking what to do, he got word that he had won the Patrick Kavanagh Award. He knew none of the judges; it was a total surprise. He decided to give the poetry another chance, to bring a book out, to work at poetry.

In 1975 *O Westport in the Light of Asia Minor* came out; *Teresa's Bar* appeared the following year; he got a bursary from the Arts Council; *Sam's Cross* came out in 1978; *Jesus, Break His Fall* in 1980; *Ark of the North* in 1982 for the eightieth birthday of Francis Stuart; *Jumping the Train Tracks with Angela* in 1984. Blackstaff Press brought out his *Selected Poems*, edited by Edna Longley, in 1982. His poems were published regularly in *Magill* and later in *In Dublin*. He wrote a column in the *Cork Examiner*. He edited several brilliant issues of the *Cork Review*. He became a member of *Aosdana*.

He became known for a certain sort of public poem, with the title like a newspaper headline, a political slogan, a parody, or a catch-phrase: 'Minister Opens New Home For Battered Husbands', 'The Head Transplant', 'Irish Hierarchy Bans Colour Photography'.

Portrait of the Artist as a Spring Lamb

When I was a boy, myself and my girl
Used bicycle up to the Phoenix Park;
Outside the gates we used to lie in the grass
Making love outside Áras an Uachtaráin.

('Making Love Outside Áras an Uachtaráin)

He became known for writing elegies for the dead: Seamus
Murphy, Cearbhall Ó Dálaigh, Sid Vicious, and poems about
the murdered dead: the Miami Showband, the victims of the
sectarian murders, those murdered in the Dublin bombings.

Next to the fresh grave of my beloved grandmother
The grave of my first love murdered by my brother.

('Ireland, 1972')

He has been introduced and spoken of as a Liverpool-type
poet, as a performing poet, as a naïve poet, a set of labels
which only serves to undermine the seriousness of his work,
and his skill.

This morning, early, I received a shock; for marriage
Is a hard life and each new winter marks
A darker degree of dark, a darker image,
Another tree-ring added to the soul's thick bark.

('She Transforms the Ruins into a Winter Palace')

He moved from publisher to publisher. When he read his
new poems, the ones published in *The Berlin Wall Café*, in
Belfast, Blackstaff immediately offered to publish them and
also issued a new edition of the *Selected Poems*. The second
half of the book was about the break-up of his marriage with
Nessa.

Dear Nessa — Now that our marriage is over
I would like you to know that, if I could put back the
    clock

Fifteen years to the cold March day of our wedding,
I would wed you again...

('Hymn to a Broken Marriage')

Publishing these poems, which dealt directly and indirectly with the break-up of the marriage, worried him. In the end he felt that it would not be destructive to his wife and his children; he wouldn't have published them had he felt otherwise. The book was the choice of the Poetry Book Society.

Yet our love-cries in the night had grown infrequent
And she multiplied the numbers of cigarettes she
* smoked,*
After she went out to work, and the children to school,
I stood in the kitchen cleaning ashtrays.

('Cleaning Ashtrays')

In 1983 he travelled to the Soviet Union with Anthony Cronin. He remembers arriving in Armenia, looking at Mount Ararat, aware that he was now in his old homeland of Asia Minor. There was a dinner, it was a great night, their host knew the work of Flann O'Brien and James Joyce. There were moments in Russian literature which were important for Paul Durcan, especially at that time the work of Pasternak: he knew the poems in *Doctor Zhivago*, as well as *Letters to My Georgian Friends* and essays by Pasternak.

After all these years, Boris Leonidovich Pasternak,
I have found you.
How self-engrossed and paranoid I must appear to you
Lurking at the foot of your grave.

A blue corduroy cap on my head
That I purchased in a West-of-Ireland village;

A green scarf tied around my throat,
A Japanese automatic camera in my hand.

('Peredelkino: at the Grave of Pasternak')

As they were flying over the Caucauses back to Moscow he looked at the mountains below and said to Anthony Cronin "Look, they look like tents." Cronin replied: "Paul, would you ever stop saying that things are like things. They either are or they're not." He has never, he says, used the word 'like' since that day. His journey to Russia was crucial for him in many ways. It seems like another time when he thinks about it. He was shocked when he came back and Reagan made his Evil Empire speech. He could talk about it all night, the events they attended in which groups of writers spoke to the two Irish poets about the Soviet Union and then listened as the two poets spoke about Ireland. He asked about Pasternak and why *Doctor Zhivago* was not in the shops, it was like throwing a broken bottle into a ring. One editor made remarks about Pasternak's personal morality, but another said that the time was not far off when he would be published

Paul Durcan went back to Leningrad for a conference of writers in 1985 and in September 1986 he went on a six-week journey. He wanted to go back and spend time there. He was trying to learn Russian. He had originally hoped to go there for six months, but the logistics and the finances were too difficult to arrange. On his second day in Moscow he heard the word "glasnost" for the first time.

Going down the airbridge, I slow my step
Savouring the moment of liberation;
As soon as I step aboard the Aeroflot airliner
I will have stepped from godlessness into faith

('Going Home to Russia')

There was a problem with his guide, with people urging him to speak his mind, and his own need to speak his mind in a political climate which was not used to that. He remembers his guide driving around the ring-roads of Moscow playing Stevie Wonder on the car cassette. He felt that his movements were being monitored, he began to feel the strain. There was serious tension when they went to Gori, the birthplace of Stalin.

> *You would imagine — would you not —*
> *That the town of Gori,*
> *The town of Joseph Vissarionovich Dzhugashvili,*
> *By virtue of being just that —*
> *Stalin's home town —*
> *Would be a self-centred, uninhabited, pock-marked*
> * crater,*
> *'The town that gave birth to...'*
> > ('The Woman with the Keys to Stalin's House')

He had got out of the car in Stalin Square in Gori, had his photograph taken underneath the statue of Stalin and barely entered the Stalin Museum when Graham Greene — whom he had also seen two days previously in a graveyard in Bellisi — came walking around the museum. He did not speak to him. The appearance of Greene in these strange places is part of the surreality of that time when he felt that his guide, on whom he was totally dependent, was trying to brain-wash him, when he felt under incredible pressure. He ended up being put on the Aeroflot plane to Shannon without his bags or his notebooks. They arrived six weeks after he did. When he came back he was, he says, really shook.

> *I am a citizen of a secret society.*
> *Although God was born in Russia*
> *It is a well-kept secret.*
> *In Red Square on Palm Sunday*

I looked through Brezhnev's eyes
When they were open, and I saw
Ten thousand secret faces wave up at me.
'Jesus, it's May Day!' he growled at me.

('Tbilisi Cabaret')

On 8 January 1988 Paul Durcan's father died. He began to write the poems which were later published in *Daddy, Daddy* in 1990. Everything came back:

There were not many fields
In which you had hopes for me
But sport was one of them.
On my twenty-first birthday
I was selected to play
For Grangegorman Mental Hospital
In an away game
Against Mullingar Mental Hospital.
I was a patient
In B Wing.
You drove all the way down,
Fifty miles,
To Mullingar to stand
On the sidelines and observe me.

('Sport')

Once more, like the poems about the break-up of his marriage, he was prepared to write about the most personal and difficult moments, and to add other moments of pure comedy and surrealism.

Daddy and I were lovers
From the beginning, and when I was six
We got married in the church of Crinkle, near Birr
The Irish Independent photographed the wedding.

My mother gave me away.
My sister was best man.

> ('Crinkle, near Birr')

In Ireland, what happens within the family remains so secretive, so painfully locked within each person, that any writer who deals with the dynamics of family life stands apart. He supported Mary Robinson during the Presidential election campaign in 1990, and spoke in her favour during a Late Late Show special on RTE. She quoted from one of his poems, 'Backside to the Wind', in her victory speech.

I met him in Drogheda in 1990 just before *Daddy, Daddy* was published. He had a copy with him, and, once more, he was worried about how it would be received. He was living near Drogheda, he made it sound like a holy refuge, a place of exile, just as he had previously done with London, Cork and Ringsend.

He liked the small towns in Ireland, enjoyed mooching around on his own in a place where no one would know him. That day we went to Newgrange. He had learned to draw every stone in the passageway. It was a place which filled him with infinite fascination and wonder.

On the banks of the Boyne on a June night,
I lie under the great snail cairn of Newgrange
Watching men go to the moon
While their women give birth to more women.
My snail-soul is light sensitive.

> ('A Snail in My Prime')

He travelled a great deal in those years, he won prizes, he won fame. The readings drained him, he put so much emotion and drama into them. He was careful not to do too many. He remained elusive and secretive, never revealing what his next project was going to be. He read a great deal — fiction, non-fiction, poetry. He was always looking for a new book, a name he didn't know. But he had a special reverence for certain painters: Francis Bacon, for example, or R B Kitaj. In 1991 he published *Crazy About Women*, poems about paintings in the Irish National Gallery.

> *My mother is as much*
> *A virgin at seventy-five*
> *As she was at seventeen;*
> *As much a small*
> *Stream going nowhere;*
> *As much a small ocean going everywhere;*
> *Terracotta moon*
> *In pink nightie.*
>
> ('The Virgin and Child, after Lorenzo Ghiberti')

In 1994, a year after *A Snail in My Prime: New and Selected Poems* had been published by Harvill, he published *Give Me Your Hand*, a book of poems about paintings in the British National Gallery. His reading, accompanied by slides of the paintings, was in a vast hall to the side of the gallery. It was booked out days in advance. For another writer this business of being at the very centre of things in Trafalgar Square, in the centre of London, in the heart of the faded Empire, with a huge audience, might mean something, and no doubt it meant a great deal to him, but there is always the sense that when he finishes a reading and goes home, he goes far back into himself.

> *If only there was just one human being out there*
> *With whom I could make a home? Share a home?*
> *Just one creature out there in the night —*
> *In Helsinki, perhaps? Or in Reykjavik?*
> *Or in Chapelizod? Or in Malahide?*
>
> ('The Centre of the Universe')

When I interviewed him first in 1986 he was living in a small house in Ringsend — soon he moved to another house in the same street. He spoke about a night when he had walked from the centre of Dublin down O'Connell Street, along Pearse Street into Ringsend, on to Pigeonhouse Road. He had been to the theatre. As he crossed the small, narrow, hump-backed bridge at Ringsend over the Dodder, night had just fallen and he looked west towards the Dublin mountains and saw the mast on top of Three Rock Mountain and he could also see the red light on the mast of Telefis Eireann.

There was a full moon over the Sugarloaf. He stood there gazing out at all of this. Out of the corner of his eye he could see the painted signs of the pubs in Ringsend, the lights. Just then, he felt more than a little troubled about a number of things. But it was a lovely warm, clear night and he was open to what he saw. If he had seen it for the first time, if this was his first time in the city, he would have seen it as just a vision of beauty, without the usual estrangement and sadness.

> *"I've become so lonely, I could die" — he writes*
> *The native who is an exile in his native land:*
> *"Do you hear me whispering to you across the Golden*
> * Vale?*
> *Do you hear me bawling to you across the hearthrug?"*
>
> ('Ireland, 1977')

Now, nine years later, he is happier. He has just been on a tour of Brazil, and soon he will go to Canada. For the next two weeks he will drive with a friend around the West of Ireland. He has left his bag in my house and he calls to collect it on his way to the West with his friend. The previous evening he has drawn my attention to a poem in *Give Me Your Hand* called 'The Mantlepiece', inspired by a painting by Vuillard, and as his friend sits on the sofa I look at her and think about the poem.

I put out a finger with which to trace the marble
But trace her instead — trace her cheekbone.
Is your mantlepiece an altar?
She smiles: Are you my spring lamb?
I am.

That was five and a half years ago.
The world that is the case is everything and new.
O my drowned spring lamb!
O my wild, wild mantlepiece!

In the Light of Things as They Are
Paul Durcan's Ireland

Fintan O'Toole

I want to live with you
In the light of things as they are;

('The Dublin-Paris-Berlin-Moscow Line')

One of the peculiarities of modern Irish culture is that there has been no real division between the mainstream and the avant-garde. Some writers have been more conservative about form than others, but on the whole Irish writing has been remarkable for the extent to which it is impossible to divide it into a mainstream that tries to reflect social reality on the one hand and an avant-garde that is concerned to explore the limits of form and language on the other. The reason is not hard to find: Irish reality has been, in a period of crisis and change, itself so angular and odd, so full of unlikely conjunctions and broken narratives, that a good realist has had to be also a surrealist. A jagged, many-layered reality has evoked from writers a protean, many-faced response. Paul Durcan is one of the few who have been able to immerse themselves in the flow of change and contradiction and still emerge with a coherent and distinctive body of work.

In the 1950s, when Paul Durcan was a child, the idea that Irish reality could be depicted only through the use of strange and surreal imagery suggested itself to many people. As emigration became a flood, people began to imagine Ireland as a place in which what was absent and unseen was as real as what was present and visible. A book called *The Vanishing Irish* suggested that soon there might be no one left on the island. A cartoon in the *Irish Times* showed one unsuccessful entrant in an Abbey playwrighting competition telling another: "I suppose my dramatisation of *The Vanishing Irish* was a bit avant-garde: just a set — no actors." Equally, in 1950, the critic Thomas Hogan wrote in *Envoy* that:

> among my unwritten plays there are two designed for what I thought would have been the finish up of the tradition of economic and relatively motionless acting. One is to be performed with a black curtain across the proscenium arch with holes cut in it so that the actors can shout their lines unwinkingly at the audience. The other presents possibly insuperable technical difficulties for it is designed for no actors at all.

Before Samuel Beckett shocked European culture with theatrical images of things that were not happening, there were people in Ireland who had images in their heads of a theatre like his, not as an exercise in the avant-garde, but as a description of reality. Irish reality itself had a surreal quality. The image of the country as a vast stage set, a cultural performance space lit by the twin glows of faith and fatherland, but with fragmented and obscure characters playing on it, seemed not like a dark absurdist fantasy, but like an only slightly exaggerated version of the real Ireland.

In 'The Persian Gulf', Paul Durcan remarks that 'Abstract Art was in Ireland long before Abstract Art', encapsulating this strange sense in which the conditions of Irish life tended to dissolve the distinction between the real and the surreal, between the aesthetic and the political. Reading Paul Durcan is like watching a continual, picaresque play on that strange stage set that Ireland became. The stage is furnished with political and religious orthodoxies, and populated with the figures that the poet has encountered in a life that is one long journey.

In 'The Only Man Never to Meet Samuel Beckett', Durcan plays on the fact that he never met Beckett, not to distance himself from the older writer, but to emphasize an affinity much deeper than personal acquaintance. There is, in Durcan's work, no meeting with Beckett, no literary influence at work. But there is something much more striking — a continual series of random encounters with Beckett's world, encounters that are not just the usual theatrical ones, but that take place on the streets, at bus-stops, in the hustle-bustle of the city. Beckett will not leave him alone:

Whispering to him: Go away.
But he'd whisper back:
Won't go away.
                    ('The Only Man Never to Meet Samuel Beckett')

The Ireland of Durcan's poems is itself so Beckettian that his meetings with Beckett are more often through life than through art. In 'The Beckett at the Gate', a visit to a Beckett show becomes the occasion for an erotic encounter with a young woman. In 'Gogo's Late Wife Tranquilla', we enter the extra-theatrical life of one of Beckett's best-known characters, as if Didi and Gogo were out there on the streets of Dublin.

And even when there is no explicit reference to Beckett, there are powerful echoes. It is not for nothing, for instance, that Durcan's poetic recreations of his own childhood read strikingly like one of Beckett's later novels. It is hard to read a poem like 'Going Home to Mayo, Winter, 1949', with its image of a boy and a man moving across a silent landscape

in a futile journey towards death without thinking of Beckett's
Worstward Ho. Durcan's

Thousands of crosses of loneliness planted
In the narrowing grave of the life of the father;
In the wide, wide cemetery of the boy's childhood

feels like Beckett's old man and boy as they 'Slowly with
never a pause plod on and never recede. Backs turned. Both
bowed. Joined by held holding hands. Plod on as one. One
shade. Another shade.'

The point of the comparison is not to suggest a literary
influence. On the contrary, Durcan's poem was published five
years before Beckett's novel. It is the much more interesting
point that the Ireland in which Paul Durcan writes lends itself
in reality to the kind of imagery that Beckett deployed
metaphorically and metaphysically. Beckett's abstract
landscape and mute, anonymous figures, become in some of
Durcan's poems, a literal landscape of named towns —
Kilcock, Kinnegad, Strokestown, Elphin — traversed by the
poet and his father. The abstract art that was in Ireland before
abstract art allows the poet to be at once literal and
metaphysical, at once a remembered self and a haunting
figure in a dark play of human isolation.

And indeed this is made more or less explicit in Durcan's
work. The idea that the Ireland of the 1950s is like a Beckett
play is suggested in 'The Beckett at the Gate':

Not since the Depression of the 1950s
And the clowns in Duffy's Circus
Have I laughed myself so sorry,
So sorry that I was ready to shout,
If anyone else had shouted:
"Stop Beckett! Stop McGovern!"

Even more explictly, 'Archbishop of Dublin to Film *Romeo and Juliet*' imagines the real, 1980s world of the Irish Catholic hierarchy's interventions into politico-sexual debates as a Beckettian drama:

The Archbishop of Dublin,
Inspired by the example of Saint Samuel Beckett
— We were told —
Will isolate Romeo and Juliet
In separate refrigerators:
Romeo in a refrigerator in Rome,
And Juliet in a refrigerator in Armagh.

These parallels with Beckett remind us that Paul Durcan's Ireland is a place at once real and absurd. For all the comic invention, all the dark exploration, of his work, Durcan is above all a great realist. He is a brilliant describer of a reality so dislocated, so imbued with political, religious and psychic myths, that it will not yield to prosaic language or to literal minds. The madness of his poetry is a realistic reflection of the mad Ireland that has stung him into it.

The realism of Durcan's work lies at one level in the simple fact that he noticed and noted more about Irish reality than most poets do. What he has noticed in particular is the gap between the way Ireland was supposed to be and the way it is. Because he is in thrall to none of the inherited orthodoxies of Irish writing — the preference for the country over the city, the belief in Ireland as a fixed frame for experience, the assumption that mundane reality is not fit material for poetry — Durcan shows a vivid awareness of social and economic realities. Two things above all lie behind his work — the rapid transformation of Ireland into an urban, industrial society in the 1960s and 1970s, and the extraordinary cultural porousness that resulted from this transformation. Paul Durcan is the poet of those fluid but inescapable facts.

The emergence of a new middle-class, whose identity is inseparable from material possessions, for instance, is captured in 'The National Gallery Restaurant':

I'd prefer to converse about her BMW — or my BMW —
Or the pros and cons of open plan in office-block
*   architecture.*

Or in 'Tullynoe: Tête à Tête in the Parish Priest's Parlour', where a dead man's life history is measured out in automobiles:

"...he was a grand man."
"He was: he had the most expensive Toyota you can
*   buy."*
"He had: well it was only beautiful."
"It was: he used to have an Audi."
"He had: as a matter of fact he used to have two
*   Audis."*

Funny as such satires are, they allude to a world that is more real than invented. It is the world of a burgeoning middle-class Ireland whose culture is displaced and whose history can only be measured by the succession of cars. And just as time has lost its bearings, place has lost its reality:

We live in a Georgian, Tudor, Classical Greek,
Moorish, Spanish Hacienda, Regency Period
Ranch-House, Three-Storey Bungalow
On the edge of the edge of town:
'Poor Joe's Row' —
The townspeople call it —
But our real address is 'Ronald Reagan Hill',
*   — That vulturous-looking man in the States.*

('The Haulier's Wife Meets Jesus on the
Road Near Moone.')

The movement of these lines, through a random succession of periods and places, through a landscape where even the names of places are unstable, where a woman starts to describe her home in Tipperary and ends up in the United States, could be called post-modern. But if Durcan is a post-modern writer, he is so for reasons far more profound than style. He writes out of a society that has become post-modern without ever really becoming modern, a place in which the global village is still a one-horse town. Durcan's Ireland is saturated with media imagery and has taken its place in cyberspace. But it is also stuck with peasant politics, an obscurantist church and with a mediaeval sectarian conflict on its doorstep.

Most powerfully, of course, this other, pre-modern Ireland is embodied for Durcan in the figure of his father. Because his father, as a judge,

> *The President of the Circuit Court*
> *Of the Republic of Ireland,*
> *Appointed by the party of Fine Gael*
> ('Poem Not Beginning With a Line from Pindar')

'served the State/ Unconditionally/ For twenty-eight years'('The Dream in a Peasant's Bent Shoulders'), there is no real dividing line between the public and private, the emotional and the political in his work. The State has for him a local habitation and a name, an intimate psychic presence that makes it far more than a collective abstraction. Public events in Ireland and elsewhere are refracted in many poems through the image of his father, the public man. In the process, Irish history becomes for Durcan both a dream and a nightmare.

As it is for Joyce's Stephen Daedalus, Irish history is for
Durcan a nightmare from which he is trying to awake. But it
is also a daydream, a wide-awake effort at re-imagining the
past. Like Stephen, Durcan is also a wanderer in search of
alternative fathers. Because his own father is both a personal
and a politicial progenitor, he looks for other fathers that
embody historic political alternatives to the Ireland we
actually got. Ireland's political father-figure, Eamon de
Valera, is pictured 'blindly stalking us down' ('Making Love
Outside Áras an Uachtaráin'). Dismissed, he is replaced by a
series of political figures with more capacity for
contradiction, less for purity. Three deaths in March 1978
provide a coincidental but nonetheless sacred trinity of
historic alternatives in Durcan's laments. Emmett Dalton,
through whom the unlikely figures of Tom Kettle dying in the
British Army in France and Michael Collins dying at *Beal na
mBlath*, are united, is one such figure. Micheál
MacLiammóir, who '...dreamed a dream of Jean Cocteau /
Leaning against a wall in Kilnamoe' is another. And the third
is Cearbhall Ó Dálaigh,

> *A Gaelic Chinaman whose birthplace*
> *At 85 Main Street, Bray,*
> *Is today a Chinese Restaurant*
> *('The Jasmine' owned by Chi Leung Nam)*

Through such figures an alternative Irish history is
imagined. But so, too, in Durcan's poems, is an alternative
Irish geography, one in which France and Cork, France and
Mayo, China and Bray, are neighbouring townlands. These
unlikely conjunctions are the alternatives to Ronald Reagan
Hill, in which the porous placelessness of modern Ireland is
re-imagined not as a cultural nightmare but as a cause for
celebration. And this is the point about Durcan's attitude to
Ireland. He does not fly from the narrowness of Irish history

or the absurdity of Irish geography. He imagines alternatives to them. And these alternatives are themselves rooted in Irish reality. They are made, not by pure invention, but by loosening the tongue of a hidden Ireland, allowing it to speak out its own unspoken complexities and richly contradictory possibilities.

This is at once an act of faith and of perception. In his foreword to Patrick Kavanagh's *Lough Derg*, Paul Durcan remarked that 'much of his work...demands of the reader spiritual courage as well as highly sensitive powers of perception...' That the same words could be used about Durcan himself is a reminder of the nature of his achievement. In his work, the power of seeing and the gift of believing go hand-in-hand. Wallace Stevens's definition of poetry as 'an interdependence of the imagination and reality as equals' comes to mind. In Durcan's work, reality is always shaped and often transformed by the imagination. But it holds its place on equal terms. All writers try not to betray their own imaginative impulses. What distinguishes Paul Durcan is that, at the same time, he tries equally not to betray reality.

He has never, for instance, followed the standard poetic belief that poetry is a kind of knowledge that is of a different order to journalistic reporting of reality. Durcan, in fact, goes very far indeed in aligning poetry with good reportage. In his early 'Tribute to a Reporter in Belfast, 1974', he not only pays homage to the work of RTE's Liam Hourican in his reports on the violence in Northern Ireland, but asks whether his 'uniquely utilitarian technique of truth-telling' might not be 'a poetry more/ than poetry is'. The question arises from a belief that language in Ireland has been abused 'and by poets as much as by gunmen or churchmen'. From this belief stems the essential commitment of all of Durcan's work — a commitment to a kind of poetry that does not abuse reality by abusing language. His quest can be said to be a search for a poetry that combines the integrity and the truth to life of the best journalism with the imaginative boldness of James Joyce or Patrick Kavanagh.

In this sense, Durcan is more concerned to describe his Ireland, to name it truthfully, than he is to poeticize it. His journalistic poems, in which he uses newspaper headlines and the form of the news report may be usually — though not always — satiric in intent. But it is always the kind of satire that conceives of itself in Swiftian terms as a magnification of reality so that we may see it the better.

The reality of Ireland is abundantly present in the poems. The most obvious thing about Durcan's work, indeed, is that in its range of both geographical and historical reference, it is unique. No living Irish poet and few dead ones can match the sheer range of Irish places reflected in the work. Three places are especially important — Dublin, Cork and Mayo — but an astonishing range of others make their presence felt. Durcan is a national poet in the simple sense that his work touches on every part of Ireland — Lisdoonvarna, Cahir, Knock, Armagh, Corofin, Belfast, Dun Chaoin, Racoo, Ballyferriter — in the process eluding the distinctions between North and South, between country and city.

In his continual naming of Irish places, Durcan is not a mere enumerator of points on a road map. Deeply embedded in his poetry is the idea that to name is to bless. In 'Amnesty', he recalls his father:

For whom the names of places and people
Are the signs by which he teaches me
That they are holy and precious;
That the plankton of all human life is mercy.

Conversely, 'a place that does not have a name' — the prison — is 'not a holy and precious place'. The naming of so many places in Durcan's poems is thus an act of blessing and of mercy imbued with an intent far beyond that of creating a recognisable backdrop. His insistent naming of places that would otherwise have remained unnamed in poetry and therefore have been denied a recognition of their preciousness is one of the most important aspects of Durcan's care for Irish reality. He is the poet who, more than any other, has invented work capacious enough to articulate within its syntax the flotsam and jetsam of an Irish reality that had no place within the rural and romantic traditions of the Irish Revival.

Who else has named in poetry 'the Asahi synthetic-fibre plant ('Backside to the Wind'), Donnybrook Garage ('Margaret, Are You Grieving?'), Marks and Spencer's ('The Repentant Peter'), the Pass Machine of the Bank of Ireland in O'Connell Street ('Exterior With Plant'), the Kentucky Grill ('Chips'), the National Gallery Restaurant, the East Link Toll Bridge ('Dairine Vanston, 1903-1988' and 'The Toll Bridge'), the Bovril Sign, the Ballast Office Clock, the Broadstone' ('Hymn to My Father')?

But Durcan is no mere poetic topographer. His Ireland is, in its own way, a holy Ireland. What makes it holy is the poet's ability to imbue its physical reality with the only blessings he knows - speech and sex. He makes Ireland both a suburb of Babel and an erogenous zone. The geography of Durcan's Ireland is the utopian geography of Joyce's *Finnegans Wake* in which Dublin is also the Dublin that is the county seat of Laurens County, Georgia, Baile Atha Cliath is also Balaclava, Dublin is also Lublin, the New Ireland is also the New Island (America), Crumlin is the Kremlin, West Munster is

Westminster and the four provinces are 'used her, mused her, licksed her and cuddled.'

Landscape, in Durcan's work, is aroused to life both by being released from the confines of physical fixity and by being eroticised. The former is a political impulse, the latter a personal one, but as usual in his work they melt into each other. In this, he reflects realistically but imaginatively, not only the facts of his own life but also the nature of contemporary Ireland as a cultural space forever hovering between America and Europe.

'In Before the Celtic Yoke', Durcan imagines a literal geography, a writing of lands, in which physical reality becomes itself articulate, with 'verbs dripping fresh from geologic epochs'. In 'The Mayo Accent', speech and land become one as:

Words are bog oak sunk in understatement;
Phrases are bog water in which syllables float...

The land is freed from the tyranny of its physical fixity and becomes ambiguous, infinitely capable of re-invention, as promiscuous and as slippery as language itself. Every place becomes sayable, every corner of Irish reality can be named, and thus find room in the utopian Babel that is Durcan's poetic homeland.

And just as Irish land can become articulate in Durcan, so too does it become imbued with sex. The landscape is frequently eroticised — perhaps the most profound mark of the influence of Kavanagh on Durcan: 'the urban necklaces far below on the breast of the coastline' ('EI Flight 106: New York to Dublin'); 'the sea's thighs pillowing in' ('Martha's Wall'); 'the hips of the Shannon estuary/ The pores of the

gooseflesh of Ireland.' ('Going Home To Russia'). In 'O
Westport in the Light of Asia Minor':

The islands come up through the mists
— Seductive garments that a man would dream of —

Just as the landscape can be humanised, so people can be
assimilated to the landscape, as Nessa is in the vision of her
as 'a whirlpool'. In 'Hymn to Nessa':

Behind me on the sea shore Nessa lay
She is the red sun at nightfall...

This may be a familiar poetic device, but it makes room for
the central achievement of Durcan's realism, his invocation
of an Ireland that is not a stable island, but a floating one. In
his roles as priest and lover, blessing places and lusting after
them, Durcan frees the land from its appearance of mute
fixity. He comes as close as anyone has to describing the real
cultural Ireland, a place that is not a point on the map, but
rather closer to that humanised map that the cartographer Tim
Robinson has described as a picture of the 'nodes at which
the layers of experience touch and may be fused together'.

Place in Durcan is unstable, permeable, unbounded.
Durcan's Ireland exists, not just in recognisable place-names,
but in such surreal but meaningful places as 'the east
European parts of Dublin city', 'the road from Mayo into
Egypt', 'Westport in the Light of Asia Minor', 'Africa on the
West Coast of Kerry', 'the Kalahari, Pimlico, and the West of
Ireland', 'The Dublin-Paris-Berlin-Moscow Line', 'a French
Ireland'.

These are the places of a poet who asks of 'the history of
transport — is there any other history?' ('Red Arrow'). For
Durcan is, supremely, the poet, not just of emigration, but of
a place constituted by its history of emigration. The American

tourists in 'Loosestrife in Ballyferriter' to whom 'Ireland is an odyssey odder than Iowa' are not too far in their sense of estrangement from a poet whose Ireland is, above all else, an odyssey, a journey, a history of transport. For not only is the Durcan of the poems continually in motion around Ireland and beyond it to Russia, America, France, Italy, Catalonia, and England, but the places themselves are continually shifting and melting into each other.

There are parallel universes on either edge of Europe, the Atlantic and the Caucusus. Poems placed in Ireland repeat themselves on the far side of Europe, as when 'The Girl With the Keys to Pearse's Cottage' becomes 'The Woman with the Keys to Stalin's House', and 'Going Home to Mayo' becomes 'Going Home to Russia'. 'Home' is neither Mayo nor Moscow but both and therefore neither:

> From the shores of the Aran Islands
> To the foothills the far side of the Caucusus
> These are the terraced streets
> That smell of home to us.
>
> ('The Dublin-Paris-Berlin-Moscow Line')

Because of his profound sense of the instability of place, Durcan writes always as an exile, even when he is at home. In 'Ireland 1977', he is 'the native who is an exile in his native land.' 'May I, a Dubliner, live always in exile', he prays in 'The Dublin-Paris-Berlin-Moscow Line'. This sense of internal exile, of being both the one who stayed and the one who went, gives Durcan a special access to emigrant Ireland, to a place that is defined by its leavetakings. He writes directly of emigration in poems like 'The Girl With the Keys to Pearse's Cottage', and 'Backside to the Wind', where there are relatively conventional if also unusually moving images of young people forced to leave the West of Ireland. But he also, less conventionally, writes about Irish emigrants as part of a 'caravan of immigrants' ('The Deep Supermarket'; 'Next Door to Ajay's'), taking their place in a migratory humanity marked 'by the relation of man and woman on this earth/ Be/ He or she/ from Mayo or Sind...' Emigration, in his work, is both a political fact and a spiritual state.

Because of emigration, Durcan's Ireland not merely has no fixed sense of place, but its history, both personal and national, is continually queasy with motion sickness. The man conceived in the toilets of the Cork-Dublin train ('The Boy Who Was Conceived in the Leithreas'), the couple making love in a Peugeot in a car wash ('High-Speed Car Wash'), the man who died falling out of train ('Tullynoe: Tête à Tête in the Parish Priest's Parlour') are emblematic figures in Durcan's Ireland, images of 'having become the migrants that we are' ('The Dublin-Paris-Berlin-Moscow Line'). In his poems, Irish life from conception to death is lived in transit. Almost every poem takes place on the hoof — walking, driving, in a train, in a foreign city. And this is what makes him the national bard of the Republic of Elsewhere of which most Irish people are citizens.

One of the few Durcan poems that takes place entirely within a house, 'Man Walking the Stairs', happens on the stairs, the part of a house given over entirely to motion.

The whole point of my home
Is the stairs. Can you conceive
Of a life without stairs?

The importance of Paul Durcan is that he can't. He lives, as a poet, neither downstairs in the foul rag-and-bone shop of the heart, nor upstairs in the realms of public history and culture, but on the stairs between them. He lives neither in the serene world of literary tradition nor in the demotic hurly-burly of sex and drugs and rock 'n' roll, but on the stairs between them. He lives neither in an immemorial Ireland of the past nor in an amnesiac Ireland of the present, but on the stairs between them. Stairs are awkward, bumpy, irregular and angular places to live on, hard to get up and easy to fall down. Paul Durcan's willingness to endure poetic life in such places makes him the man with the keys to the Irish tower of Babel.

Prime Durcan: A Collage

Eamon Grennan

Seeing Things

Leaving an art gallery or museum of art after looking at paintings for a couple of hours, I often find I'm seeing the world differently, at least for a little while. I notice the shapes and volumes of things — all those cones and pyramids, oblongs and triangles that the things of the world can render down to. I see with a revived eye the extraordinary fact of colour in the world — those glints of gold and silver in a sea of green grass, the way a window can be an explosion of turquoise when the sun hits it, the black, maroon and magenta geometry of a woman's scarf as it curls across her shoulder, the intense vitality of yellow in a twist of lemon peel, the cat's malachite eyes. It isn't just a case of life imitating art. It's more a question of the inspired and calculated facts of art waking us up to the vast particularity of things, to the infinite dazzle of their surfaces as well as to the sensuous, indefinable order that seems to inhere in them. Most of all, I suppose, it is a question of briefly seeing the world through the painters' eyes: the world will take its cue from the painters I've been especially impressed with, will look back at me in the way I imagine it must have looked to their interrogative and creative gaze.

Something analogous to this happens to me after I've been reading a lot of Paul Durcan's poetry. I start to see the world at the Durcan angle. Things I would not normally pay much attention to begin to strike me as slightly bizarre. The world, like Aliceland, grows curiouser and curiouser. Recently, for example, while reading Durcan's work for this essay, I attended a concert by an American-Irish music group called Celtic Thunder. Their fiddle player is an Asian-American, David Abe, and their pianist, Regan Wick, mixes jazz improvisation with Irish melodies. This young man is also a champion step-dancer and his high leaps in the middle of a reel or a hornpipe brought thoughts of Nijinsky and Birdman Sweeney to mind. I say I attended the concert; in fact I gave a reading before the music, so the flyer for the evening read 'Eamon Grennan Followed by Celtic Thunder', a stage direction to challenge 'Exit pursued by Bear'. The next day I went to a concert given by the South African *a capella* singing group, Ladysmith Black Mombasa, whose striking mixture of individuality and community in their singing, as well as the astonishing spectacle of their "tiptoe guys" dancing (a form of Saturday night silent hopping and kicking developed by the miners to elude the detection of guards in their camps) which fused energy and constraint in spellbinding ways. Their bright shirts, dashikis — brilliant lozenge patterns on an amber ground — reminded me of vestments on figures in illuminated Irish manuscripts. And the other night, while taking a taxi home from the train station, I told my driver — a Jamaican — I was from Ireland. "My grandfather's Irish," he said, "his parents came over from Ireland with him. My name's MacMorris." So there I was driving down Main Street in Poughkeepsie with this gentle young black man of Irish descent, and thinking of his splenetic namesake in Shakespeare's *Henry V* — the Irish Captain MacMorris — who has this to say of his native land: 'My nation! What ish my nation? Ish a villain, and a bastard, and a knave, and a rascal — what ish my nation? Who talks of my nation?'

The confluence of these events — which under other circumstances I might not have paid much attention to — made me think I was living in a Durcan poem. Which in turn made me consider, a little enviously, what Durcan would *do* with such material. For, as a poet, he seems to live in constant touch with such slightly skewed spins on normal reality. When he holds more or less ordinary events up to the light, they glow in odd ways, revealing facets of meaning most of us could never imagine. It is his genius to discover the truly peculiar soul in things, and to celebrate or castigate this as its moral nature demands. (Although he has been called a great comedian, he is in fact a relentless — and relentlessly buoyant — moralist: weird as its projections are, the map he makes of the world is a moral map, his tendencies as a poet instinctively utopian.)

Incidents such as those I've just mentioned remind me that I know of no other poet who can do Durcan's sort of poetic justice to the *connections* offered us by everyday life, the kind of ordinary weirdnesses thrown up by our own unremarkable experience. These events were not particularly exceptional in themselves: they were marked by a certain amount of coincidence, I suppose, and a measure of the unexpected. In essence they embodied an idea of *conjunction*: conjunction within the phenomena themselves (the Asian-American playing the Irish fiddle, the Jamaican with the unlikely Irish grandfather), and a related kind of conjunction created by the observing mind (associating the South African singers with illuminated pages in the Book of Kells). Durcan's poems exist in a region ruled by this dual idea of conjunction, speaking out of it in a poetic dialect that is unmistakably his own.

Because I'd been reading him, I noticed things as I did. His poems transformed the way I saw, thought about, understood the world. Only the strongest poetry has such powers of transformation. Some poetry, pretending to such power, tries to enforce transformation, bullying us to see the world as its maker sees it. Poetry like Durcan's, however, has transformation as an involuntary by-product. It works on us in the same way as a visit to an art gallery does. When we enter the actual world again after looking at the work of a painter we love, the world (so known, so new) takes our eye by surprise. Likewise, when we've been reading Durcan for a while our world loses its steadiness and familiarity, to become a place unchanged in its essence but shaken now by comic fits and unexpected perplexities, simply riddled with astonishment.

Things Past

I remember something of those early days in UCD, when Durcan arrived in 1961 or '62 and met up with the poets there — with Macdara Woods, John Moriarty, Michael Hartnett, Michael Smith. I remember something of the aura that hung around him — something at once gloomy and bright and unpredictable. And I remember how, once, he emerged through blue clouds of cigarette smoke and a Babel-stew of talk in Dwyer's pub at the corner of Leeson Street and St Stephen's Green, beamed up close at me in a way that Guinness had something to do with — his curly hair tousled, his face bony, aquiline, hugely smiling — and shouted, *a propos* a line in a poem of mine that had just appeared in a college magazine, "Eamon, you're a saint! you're a *saint!*" and then vanished back into the scrum of drinkers and roarers, leaving me to wonder why I'd been thus canonised. The line in question, I remember, described a dead woman in her coffin being 'rolled like a stone to the tomb', and I think the simile caught his fancy, as well as the sound, maybe, and the rhythm. But it's his impulsive generosity and enthusiasm that keep the moment alive in my memory — that hearty willingness to praise, as well as the odd, wildly extravagant terms of the praise itself.

As for the poems of his that I saw at that time — pieces he published in *St Stephen's* or the *University Review* — I recall nothing but their generalised atmosphere of melancholy, the slightly exotic air of their gestures. I haven't got a copy of *Endsville* (which was published by Michael Smith's New Writer's Press in 1967), but I suppose the one poem from it that appears in *A Snail in My Prime: New and Selected Poems* (1993) is a representative sample of the early work:

Of my love's body I think
That it is a white window.
Her clothes are curtains:
By day drawn over
To conceal the light;
By night drawn back
To reveal the dark.

What I'd notice about this now is the deliberate clarity of the saying. There's a kind of purposeful plainness about the statements, in spite of the oddly impacted syntax of the first two lines, the surprising main image itself, and the enigmatic meaning of 'the dark'. The manner suggests a politely meticulous speaker who's keen to convey his meaning — to communicate — in as precise, immediate, and unambiguous a way as possible. And no matter how richly complicated, how difficult, or how intellectually and emotionally various Durcan's subsequent poems and their meanings become, I'd be inclined to say that this well-mannered wish for plain communication underlies all his work. Like a traveller returned from strange parts, he is always concerned to share the nature of the journey and the true state of where he's been.

Old Hat

What follows are excerpts from pieces I've written about Durcan's work over the years:

'Observe, too, Paul Durcan becoming one of the most original Irish poetic voices, doodling in the margins of *Teresa's Bar* — Celtic crossed with Marvel Comics.' ('A View from the Bridge: Irish Writing 1977-78', *Eire-Ireland* XIII 1978)

For all the outrage, desperation and darkness of its content, anatomising public and private ills in a language of startling directness — comic, pathetic and angry by turns or all at once — *The Berlin Wall Café* is a tonic, an exhilaration, a surge of imaginative energy as irrepressible as whatever manages, when we're stormbeaten, to keep us going. Putting on voice after voice as if they were hats (a wife, a lover, a priest, a Catholic father, a melancholy Russian, the perturbed son of a man with five penises, a witness to loving anarchy, a loutish businessman, a gas-meter man who thinks 'it would be/ Uplifting to meet the Dalai Lama', various newscasters, a loving, distressed, penitent husband, and others), Durcan reminds me of the Fool in *King Lear* — trying to make sense of the storm, mocking the world of respectable corruptions, keeping the rest of us in our right senses. The poems are clownscripts in deadly earnest, by means of which the poet enters the disastrous world of men and women at the mercy of one another or bullied by the various life-denying hypocrisies-in-residence of Church and State. Maybe Durcan is, as he's been called, a visionary poet. Certainly there are moments of exalted vision to be found here (the naked happy anarchy of the 'Man Smoking a Cigarette in the Barcelona Metro', for example, or the moving applause for fathers in '10:30 a.m. Mass, June 16, 1985'), but it seems better to call Durcan a great listener. His best achievement, it seems to me, is to put our lives into recognisable speech, speech that rollercoasts between the weird and the familiar, now brazenly colloquial, now ringing with echoes of literary tradition.

Mainly spoken in a voice that is as close to Durcan's "own" as we're likely to get, the poems in the marriage section of *The Berlin Wall Café* add up to an extended penitential elegy for what was once whole and is now broken. In these poems Durcan gives a fresh twist to the term 'confessional poetry'. According to Kavanagh, verse was the only place where a man could confess with dignity. Durcan carries this a stage further by dismantling and casting out that dangerous category — dignity. And perhaps the most remarkable fact about these surprising and disturbing confrontations with the accidents and essence of marriage is that they make successful use of some of the comic forms of drama and dramatic narrative which the poet uses for those poems dealing with the public domain, encircling them with an intensity of personal feeling and private revelation sharper and deeper than any he has touched before...These poetic anatomies of love, marriage and family are the most extraordinary utterances on the subject yet to have appeared in Irish poetry, nor do I know anything in modern British or American poetry to put beside them. In them, Durcan has found a strange, satisfying way to perform the full range of his feelings — to go public with them, to dramatise them, and at the same time to convince of their absolute privacy, their intimate actuality. Allegorical of the woe and wonder that is in marriage, the poems are also a stunning explication of the one unique, unrepeatable relationship between this man and this woman.

No one in contemporary Irish poetry has been 'gifted with so fine an ear' for the sound of Irish speech. I imagine him as sired, in this respect, by Kavanagh, by Myles na gCopaleen, and by Joyce: Kavanagh for the plain speech, the tune on a slack string; Myles for the wicked exactitudes, the deadpan scenarios that get weirder and weirder; and Joyce for the energy and variety of it all, and for the way that speech reveals consciousness.

Some of the poem-scripts don't seem animated by a core of necessary drama and so, like jokes told before, don't outlast their telling ('The Man with Five Penises', for example, or 'Archbishop of Dublin to Film Romeo and Juliet', or the soberer 'Bob Dylan Concert at Slane, 1984'). And sometimes Durcan doesn't seem quite to know how to end a poem: otherwise strong and surprising pieces like 'Girls Playing with Boys' or 'The Pietá's Over' or 'On Falling in Love with a Salesman in a Shoeshop' sort of trail off at the end in an indecisive way. But these are small faults in a collection that's a triumph of coherence, of feeling, of language, and of style. ('The Community and the Individual', *The Honest Ulsterman*, 81, 1986)

"When I read or hear the poems of Paul Durcan, it is like listening to a man standing at a boundary and, in the accents of a refugee or a displaced person, crying out over our arbitrary world of borders — whether those borders are sexual, political, tribal, social, or geographical. I read his poems as scripts which — with something of the buoyant anarchy and anarchic buoyancy of Chagall, that painter's wild and sudden and loving *weightlessness* — undermine and rearrange our fixed, that is bounded, sense of the way things are. In his ventriloquent voices I hear the Cumaean Sibyl or the Hag of Beare speaking in the common-place and contemporary Irish accents of the chapel, the pub, the office, or the shopping mall. And, good satirist that he is, he is always writing love poems — scolding and loving, trying to chant the borders down. He is a denouncer of boundaries, demotic prophet of a world without them." (Introduction to a 1992 Durcan Reading at the 92nd Street YMCA in NYC.)

To get a little closer to Durcan's specific poetic effects, I'll concentrate on a couple of features that first affect me when I read individual poems: metaphor, and the poem's movement...Probably the first things that strike me about Durcan's metaphors are their extremity, their extravagance, their naïve and 'primary' air. Here are some random examples:

> *Swags of red apples are his cheeks;*
> *Swags of yellow pears are his eyes;*
> *Foliages of dark green oaks are his torsos;*
> *And in the cambium of his bark juice lies.*

> ('Polycarp')

And I'd sit in her lap with my hands
Around her waist gulping her down
And eating her green apples
That hung in bunches from her thighs
And the clusters of hot grapes between her breasts.

('Fat Molly')

Under her gas meter I get down on my knees
And say a prayer to the side-altars of her thighs
And the three-light window of her breasts.

('The Day Kerry Became Dublin')

I turn about and see
Over the windowpane's frosted hemisphere
A small black hat sail slowly past my eyes
Into the unknown ocean of the sea at noon.

('Hat Factory')

What all these passages have in common is their benign violence of metaphorical language. In each case Durcan deliberately transfigures the world normally seen, so that it embodies a truth higher or deeper than the one on usual view. In each case the means are simple: the subject becomes something else — an orchard, an oakwood, a fruitful feast, a chapel, a flying ship, an unknown ocean. Stated as fact, none of these 'vehicles' is odd or esoteric in itself. In fact, there's an almost childlike naïveté about them. Addressed initially more to the eye than the mind, these images speak to something or somewhere quite primitive in us, full of primary colors and sensations (red, yellow, green; bunches, clusters; hot; slowly). When you consider what is being described in such terms, however (a male or female body, a hat, daylight), then the extravagant nature of this 'simplicity' (underlined by the undemanding grammatical and syntactical forms, which put no impediments between utterance and understanding) strikes home. In an act of joyous subversion, these figures of speech unmake and then remake the known world...Insisting on something deeper than the factual layer of reality we call history, they proclaim the truth of possibility, of sensual and emotional possibility. They make a world that surprises us, that shocks us into an awareness of such possibility. The fusion of extravagance and naïveté is designed not only to awaken us to a refreshed version of the world we conventionally inhabit, but to coax us to embrace the possibility of this new world in ourselves: how can it not be within our grasp when it appears, is offered, in such a simple, almost childlike way? This is how the world could be, were we rightly awake. So something of an evangelical tilt determines metaphors like this, a fact that, if recognised, might open up the otherwise encumbering notion of Durcan's being a 'visionary'. Metaphors such as those quoted above give concrete point to Derek Mahon's observation that Durcan is 'a seeker and, in Rimbaud's sense, a seer'. What Durcan sees is a world transformed, released from the old limiting laws of singular, inflexible actuality.

I would say there is something of Chagall (also a seer) in Durcan's habits of metaphor, in the way the ordinary world (its ordinariness known in the plain, colloquially direct, uncomplicated language) is altered to become a zone of metamorphic energies. In this colorful and kinetic transfiguration of the world by the word, Durcan activates a Blakean (or, nearer home, a Bloomian) hope for an existence that is all positive energy, all flow, all active peace. As invocations of a latent and fertile goodness in the natural possibility of the world (though human nature, not Nature, is Durcan's subject), these metaphors and their like are an attempt to insert that possibility into the damaged realm of the actual (and a way of fusing, maybe, the spirits of Kavanagh and Austin Clarke). Such metaphors achieve some of the same or similar effects as do Chagall's disturbances of gravity and expectation, his running together of lyrical, narrative, and autobiographical elements, his political gestures that are at once intimate and expansive. (See, for example, Chagall's The Painter and His Wife [1969], The Martyr [1939], or Around Her [1945].)

As with Chagall, too, the effect of many such metaphors in Durcan is celebratory. Both artists (at their different levels of sheer achievement) embody the extravagance of secular prayer in the comic mode. In work like this the world is renewed, liberated, made over in imagination; the distance between indicative and optative moods is eliminated. In deference to the larger laws of feeling, the old binding laws of nature are suspended. Both Chagall's amazing collocations and Durcan's metaphors testify to this truth of imagination, and the innocent force of their desire is underlined by a kind of naïve awkwardness that marks the style in each case, granting, I suppose, further proof of its sincerity. The way Chagall invites us to look at a painting may help in the reading of a typical piece of Durcan metaphor-making like the following:

> *Our children swam about our home*
> *As if it was our private sea,*
> *Their own unique, symbiotic fluid*
> *Of which their parents also partook.*
> *Such is home — a sea of your own —*
> *In which you hang upside down from the ceiling*

With equanimity, while postcards from Thailand on the
   mantlepiece
Are raising their eyebrow markings benignly:
Your hands dangling their prayers to the floorboards of
   your home,
Sifting the sands underneath the surfaces of
   conversation,
The marine insect life of the family psyche.

("'Windfall', 8 Parnell Hill, Cork')

The extended life of this metaphor is characteristic of Durcan's procedures in a number of ways. The fairly simple transforming turn of the first two lines ('swam...as if...sea') is more and more twisted as the passage continues, implicating more and more elements; the image gains a life of its own, and we are, as we are in a painting by Chagall, in a realm that hesitates between the borders of allegory and dream. The passage from 'Our children swam about our home' to 'The marine insect life of the family psyche' is a gradual thickening of metaphor, the poet's own surrender to its generative logic. And, as in the earlier examples, the metaphor is an expression of difference, the poet's way of putting an emotional truth that defies or simply eludes more rootedly normative habits of expression. The nature and activity of Durcan's metaphor, that is, imply and give solid body to a hope in the (otherwise inexpressible) spiritual and emotional dimensions of ordinary experience. Indeed, as the ordinary is luminously opened up (deepened, set flowing), spiritual and emotional dimensions are made one, identified. Metaphors like this are Durcan's way of getting beyond the limits of representation and touching those of revelation. Among other things, his metaphors are his poetic acts of faith, hope, and charity.

A poetic world of such extremities and such simplicities as those constituted by Durcan's metaphors seems designed to make us see our experience with newborn eyes — newborn, that is, in spirit and in feeling. Whether his subject is autobiographical or political, private or public, the nature of his metaphors will always attack those outworn, conventional, and spiritlessly habitual ways of receiving experience that are the death alike of public and private life — of our life as citizens and as beloved and loving creatures. In this way, Durcan's metaphors are at the single root of his double being as a poet, equally fundamental to his satires and his celebrations. They are proclamations of a different world, a world in which good and evil, joy and sorrow, are tangible absolutes, actors in a perpetual psychomachia where — as he says of 'the dark school of childhood' — 'tiny is tiny, and massive is massive' ('En Famille, 1979').

What I am calling the 'movement' of Durcan's poems is another of the elements that first compels my attention as a reader. I am intrigued by the way a poem opens, proceeds, concludes; how it gets from point to point; how it charts its course. Reading it, listening to it, I am struck by how, in spite of its quick and often surprising shifts of direction, I never lose my way. I am interested in the way the poem can contain a narrative, but how the narrative is usually absorbed by, dissolved in, the narrator's feelings (exalted, lyrical, dejected, angry, satirical) about the story being told. This conjunction of story and feelings about it (a condition that also seems to underlie formal and substantive qualities in the painting of Chagall) gives an oddly radial quality to many of the poems. Images and metaphors generate digressions, and this trajectory of movement (an operation on and in space) in turn produces a peculiar tempo (operation on and in time). So one is never lulled or (as in the case of a Heaney poem) assuaged or allured by a poem of Durcan's. Rather one is always conscious, sometimes uneasily, of being moved (in many ways) from one point or area (or emotion or conviction) to another.

Since this feature of a poem cannot be discussed in excerpts, I will use 'On Seeing Two Bus Conductors Kissing Each Other in the Middle of the Street' by way of illustration:

Electricity zig-zags through me into the blue leatherette
And I look around quick and yes —
All faces are in a state of shock:
By Christ, this busride
Will be the busride to beat all busrides.

Sure enough the conductor comes waltzing up the
*   stairs —*
The winding stairs —
And he comes up the aisle a-hopping and a-whooping
So I take my chance
Being part of the dance:
I say: 'A penny please.'
'Certainly, Sir' he replies
And rummages in his satchel
Until he fishes out a tiny penny,
An eenshy-weenshy penny,
Which he hands me crooning —
'That's especially for you Sir — thank you, Sir.'

So there it is, or was:
Will the day or night ever come when I will see
Two policemen at a street corner caressing each other?

Prime Durcan: A Collage

Let the prisoners escape, conceal them in a sunbeam?
O my dear Guard William, O my darling Guard John.

With the title as a springboard, the poem gets off to a flying start. The first stanza plunges us into the speaker's responses to this curious event. The movement is from stimulus to response to observation to further response (electricity, look, faces, exclamation). Speed is intensified by spoken immediacy, accentuated by the present tense, the 'yes', the impulsive 'By Christ' (apt, as it turns out, in a tract on brotherly love), and the enthusiastically colloquial 'busride to beat all busrides'. The movement is itself a quick zig-zag and obliges us to wonder, "What next?" We realize we are in the grip of a hectic teller of tales.

The first six lines of the next stanza form the next phase. Again the movement of the sentence — broken into metrically uneven lines that respond to the segment-logic of the phrase, the telling breath — is a speedy zig-zag, marked by loud rapid rhythmic action (waltzing, a-hopping, a-whooping) and assisted subliminally by the parenthetical reminder of the winding stairs. Quick, slightly crazy and maybe-not-there-at-all references (to Yeats in 'winding stairs' and 'part of the dance', to the marriage ceremony in 'up the aisle') further make the movement helter-skelter, yet always forward, coming to rest in the distinct, simple, actual request 'A penny please' (what the passenger normally says — or used to say when 'a penny' could still buy a bus-ticket, an archaic economic fact that Durcan may be making part of his comedy).

The normality of this exchange ('"Certainly, Sir," he replies') then swerves swiftly into the anarchic event, described, however, in a perfectly straightforward anecdotal manner: the conductor, instead of taking, gives the narrator-passenger a penny. By this time the world is topsy-turvy, but then there is yet another curve, into the parenthetical baby-talk ('eenshy-weenshy') that retards the narrative but heightens the comic suspense. Finally, the comedy crests over the crooning gesture and the extravagantly solicitous manner. As a reader I'm being presented here, at high speed, with a series of most unlikely occurrences - all unlikely because (because!) they are so expressively charitable. The speed and dodgy trace of the narrative hide its satire in strangeness: awakened by comedy I find — through this rapid mental run-around — that the point is satirical.

The final stanza steps back from the comic event to make the satiric point more decisive, and the reader has to leave the field of narrative and enter a more speculative zone. In the longer, steadier lines, movement slows to a more meditative pace, then veers into the subversive possibility of two policemen (more sinister embodiments of authority than the bus conductors) 'caressing each other'. This in turn — by means of a grammatical and syntactical skidding that, unusual in Durcan, reminds me of Muldoon — moves into a sort of prayer, thence to a dramatised exchange (but who speaks?) of erotic endearments between the two solidly named Guards. And then, suddenly and surprisingly, it is over.

Even in this brisk description it's easy to see that the movement of the whole poem is rapid and dashing — harelike in shifting direction, yet always advancing to its proper end. In such a movement, I suspect Durcan is appropriating something of the performative skill of the oral poet, who can preserve a spine of anecdotal purpose while swerving through strange, abrupt, not immediately explicable transitions. The presence of the speaking performer is what gives unity (and its own acceptable logic) to this variety and speed. And it is this (imagined) speaking presence that makes such movement real and convincing, tuning me (as I listen to the 'script') to the subversive satire of the poem even before I begin to deal with it in a more analytical way. The poem's movement, that is, exercises a primary (and — given the suggestion of orality — primitive) power, bringing me to a sort of precognitive understanding. By responding to it in this way I am participating in its comic anarchy in — from the conventional point of view — a dangerous way.

In metaphor and movement, then, Durcan's work manifests a drive toward a different world of expanded moral, spiritual, and emotional consciousness. Even at its most private (as in the marriage poems) it can be a public exhortation toward renewal. This condition is identified and aspired to by means of radical satire and celebration, by comic subversion and high but basically simple rhetorical gesture. Both metaphor and movement, at the centre of his work as I see it, show the work to be a creative attempt to bully, lovingly, the Republic into becoming a different world. In the animated metaphors and the restless movement of these poems it is possible to detect — through the oddly commanding voice of a comic scapegoat — an enterprising, surprising, courageous drive toward grace. In Durcan's way of 'being present' he performs an important job for and in Irish poetry and, more largely, Irish life. As vividly as any, his poetry shows one of the possibilities for a rich and complicated connection between the two.

Nourishment: Kavanagh, Keats *(Keats!?)*

The influence of Kavanagh is two-fold: formal and
substantive. It affects the way the poems take shape, and it
affects the way Durcan sees, takes in, and speaks back to the
world. From Kavanagh comes a trust for the actual and the
ordinary, as well as the courage to see that love can inhere in
the actual and the ordinary. An originating text could be
Kavanagh's 'The Hospital':

> *A year ago I fell in love with the functional ward*
> *Of a chest hospital: square cubicles in a row,*
> *Plain concrete, wash basins — an art lover's woe,*
> *Not counting how the fellow in the next bed snored.*

A great many of the qualities of this sonnet find their way into
Durcan's verse, among them the vision it contains (whereby
the most mundane facts of material life — ungilded by
sentimentality or 'art' — take on an edge of radiance, an aura
of spiritual importance), and the casual colloquialism of the
language itself, which is the perfectly apt expression of that
vision. In addition there's the humour ('how the fellow in the
next bed snored'), the eye for unremarkable detail.

There are differences, of course. Kavanagh, for example,
often relied formally, as he does here, on the compact
enclosure of the sonnet to give coherent and satisfying shape
to his experience. Durcan (with the exception of his
idiosyncratic engagement with the ballad tradition), is much
more thoroughly committed to the open form, letting the
material — and perhaps the requirements of the speaking
voice — give shape to the poem. (The open form itself,
however, may owe something to Kavanagh's own practise in
The Great Hunger, while both poets took instruction in the
use of supple open forms from modern American poetry).

Another difference is that Kavanagh is much more conservative in his use of image and implication. One can only imagine, for example, what Durcan would do with the suggestions built into the language of the first line and a half of 'The Hospital', how he might follow to much wilder and weirder extremes the hint of that unusual passion and the bland normality of its phrasing ('I fell in love with the functional ward of a chest hospital...'). Yet, even with such differences, it is easy to see why Durcan should say that Kavanagh was one of two artists who "changed everything for me," teaching him "that life was fundamentally good...that there was nothing that was not fit matter for a poem...and that poetry was most nearly poetry when it was most nearly prose." (Interview with Mary Dalton, *Irish Literary Supplement, Fall 1991, p. 20*)

Durcan's sense of the goodness of life comes through everywhere: even his satire and his elegies are celebratory acts. But while the initial stimulus for this is admittedly triggered by Kavanagh, the shape it achieves is very different from that given to it by the older poet. For Kavanagh located this celebratory force in himself, in his recovered or remembered response to aspects of the natural world like the Canal, in his own capacity to find a kind of Zen passivity and a capacity for praise ('So be reposed and praise, praise praise/ The way it happened and the way it is'). The locus of Kavanagh's freedom (and the source of his conviction about the goodness of life) is this admitted self — which is, however, only 'a single item in the picture', is a self freed from selfishness. This ability to be and celebrate an unabashed self (even if it leads to that dead end which Kavanagh himself hit as a poet, as the last pieces in the *Collected Poems* suggest) is what liberated Irish poetry after Kavanagh in inestimably valuable ways. While Durcan absorbed that influence, however, he avoided its more dangerous consequences by refusing to remain in the glasshouse of the self. His conviction of life's goodness has an extraordinarily broad application. His celebrations always reach deliberately beyond the self to the other, validating lives outside his own.

Kavanagh's pioneering post-romanticism — his acceptance not only of the local and the ordinary but also of the contradictory self — might be described in Keats's term, 'Negative capability... that is, when a man is capable of being in uncertainties, mysteries, doubts, without any irritable reaching after fact and reason.' (*Letters* Dec 22, 1817.) 'The day I walked out on Reason', says Kavanagh, 'was the best day of my life.' And 'To Hell with commonsense', he says, and 'to hell/ With all reasonable/ Poems in particular', for the soul needs to be honoured with 'arguments that cannot be proven'. In the Irish tradition, this willingness to exist in doubt and uncertainty is the necessary counterpoint to Yeatsian certainties, to the magnificent prejudices that hammered Yeats's extraordinary body of work into a unity Kavanagh could never achieve. By establishing this decisive break with Grandfather Yeats, however, Kavanagh fathers a great deal of contemporary Irish poetry, his line most easily traced, I'd say, into the very different work of Heaney and of Durcan.

In Durcan, Kavanagh's version of 'negative capability' leads to a much more robustly dramatised self than anything in the older poet. In fact, it might be said that what Durcan adds to the concept of negative capability is, consciously or unconsciously, Keats's own notion of 'the poetical Character': 'It is not itself — it has no self — It is everything and nothing — It has no character — it enjoys light and shade; it lives in gusto, be it foul or fair, high or low, rich or poor, mean or elevated... A poet is the most unpoetical of anything in existence, because he has no identity — he is continually in for and filling some other body...the poet has...no identity — he is certainly the most unpoetical of all God's creatures...When I am in a room with people,...the identity of every one in the room begins to press upon me, so that I am in a very little time annihilated — not only among men; it would be the same in a nursery of children...If a Sparrow come before my Window, I take part in its existence and peck about the gravel' (*Letters,* Oct 27, 1818; Nov 22 1817).

This ability to leave the self and totally inhere in another existence is surely what enables those poems in which Durcan inhabits character dramatically, becoming a multitude of perfectly realized voices, among them the voice of Ireland 'Before the Celtic Yoke', or that of the archbishop 'dreaming of the harlot of Rathkeale', or the inimitable ballad whisper of 'The Kilfenora Teaboy':

> *Oh indeed my wife is handsome.*
> *She has a fire lighting in each eye,*
> *You can pluck laughter from her elbows*
> *And from her knees pour money's tears;*
> *I make all my tea for her,*
> *I'm her teaboy on the hill,*
> *And I also thatch her roof;*
> *And I do a small bit of sheepfarming on the side.*

An essential list of these voices would also include Micheál Mac Liammóir, Sister Agnes writing home about the reverend mother's pregnancy, the middle-class male horrors who speak such poems as 'That Propellor I left in Bilbao' and 'Charlie's Mother', or the amazing recitative between the parish priest of Tullynoe and his housekeeper. Further underlining the poet's surrender to otherness, a great many of these voices are women, among them 'The Woman Who Keeps her Breasts in the Back Garden', the upper-middle-class affectation of the woman who asks 'What Shall I Wear, Darling, to *The Great Hunger*?', and — most astonishingly rich and strange — the Haulier's wife who meets Jesus 'On the Road Near Moone,' and that magnificent monologist from the dead, the nun who tells the story of 'Six Nuns Die in Convent Inferno':

> *How lucky I was to lose — I say, lose — lose my life.*
> *It was a Sunday night, and after vespers*
> *I skipped bathroom so I could hop straight into bed*
> *And get in a bit of a read before lights out.*

Revealing 'the poetical character', this inhabiting of other beings is itself also a kind of negative capability, a deliberate *dramatising* of negative capability. Since Kavanagh could only *lyricise* his negative capability, and reflect on it, Durcan's invention of a world of other voices shows how he absorbs and amplifies towards his own unique ends those inclusive lessons of attention and generosity which he learned from his master.

Coming from the Pictures

Durcan's dramatising capacity (which makes many of the poems feel less like conventional 'dramatic monologues' than like miniature scripts) is also what makes possible all those poems he has written on/after paintings — most notably in the two collections *Crazy About Women* (1991) and *Give Me Your Hand* (1994). With growing (and outrageous) authority, these poems are another sign in Durcan of Keats's 'poetical character'. For in them the poet usually inhabits one of the figures in a painting, frequently a minor figure or detail, and from this locus of identity speaks some peculiar revelation, most often at a blindingly oblique angle to what would normally be seen in (and as) the painting itself. Rubens' great 'Samson and Delilah', for example, opens in the following startling way: 'I am a master barber/ Trained in Cleveland Ohio,/ Working in Antwerp, Belgium...' Sometimes the speaker even exists outside but in some decisive relationship with the painting, as in 'A Cornfield with Cypresses', which begins, 'Let me make no bones about A Cornfield with Cypresses — / Make clear straightaway who I am./ I am the painter's mother.' Seen in the light of Keats's concept of 'poetical character', the paintings become Durcan's way away from the self, although this not-self can utter in oblique or direct ways many of Durcan's own recurrent preoccupations, as these have been gleaned from poems in 'his own' voice. (That voice, too, of course, is itself a kind of dramatised fiction, another example of 'poetical character': there is always a sense of some gap between the speaker of *any* poem and the actual Paul Durcan, a gap of a sort that Kavanagh — except to some degrees in his satires — doesn't manage. This is true even in the poems that record the breakdown of Durcan's marriage, in his own and others' voices. The experience has been *rendered* in some way, making him and his wife figures in a landscape of parable.)

One of the things that interests me in the way Durcan treats paintings he makes poems from is how the treatment is at once subjective and objective. On the one hand, the picture is inhabited as Keats inhabits the sparrow pecking about the gravel. But there's a sense in which the painting is also obliterated by what Durcan speaks out from the interior, speaks out of what he finds there for himself. So, in one of his best poems of this kind, 'The Riding School' (on the painting by Karel Dujardin), he speaks in the voice of the groom in the painting, but his subject has become art and the Northern violence ('My song is nearing the end of its tether;/ Lament in art whose end is war'), neither of which could be seen as 'belonging' to Dujardin's work . And so, in 'Lady Mary

Wortley Montagu' he speaks in the voice of the lady's clavicytherium ('My role each evening/ To stand nude in the bay window'), while Joshua Reynolds' portrait of General Sir Banastre Tarleton gives rise to a meditation in the voice of the subject's father on his son's prowess as a rugby player and his death from Aids. People and things are given voices in these poems, voices that grant life and expression to an assortment of curious existences. By his simultaneous commitment both to subjective and objective truths, it might be said that what Durcan is doing here is letting the artist, the poet, function as an agent of liberation. For the existences in question, which belong to the paintings which trigger the poems, are in a sense set free — by the poem's independent voice — of the enclosure into which the original work of art has confined them, to which it has abandoned them.

Ideas such as these may allow us to see the 'painting-poems' — so idiosyncratic, so astonishing in their inventiveness, their humour, their often powerful seriousness — as a sign of Durcan's conception of art, a conception of art which is a development of Kavanagh's aesthetic. For that aesthetic refused the sense of enclosure, wanted desperately to break down the sense of artifact as an exclusive space, a confinement, a Grecian Urn or a golden bird, wanted to make art in some way coterminous with life. 'A man, (I am thinking of myself)', says Kavanagh — in what Durcan has described as 'one of the holy texts,' the 'Author's Note' to his *Collected Poems* — 'innocently dabbles in words and rhymes and finds that it is his life.' So Durcan, by breaking into the sacrosanct enclosure of the paintings, is freeing something he has found there, something latent in the artwork itself, something that illustrates his conviction about the continuum between art and life. By extending Keats's notions of 'poetical character' and 'negative capability', mediated as they were through something indispensable in Kavanagh, Durcan in these painting-poems (as well as in other areas of his work) manages to establish an aesthetic of his own, which might be loosely described as an amplified poetics of the common touch. In the modern Irish tradition, Kavanagh inaugurates this tendency by his deliberate movement away from the language manners of Yeats and the Revival. Durcan carries this movement even further — by populating his poems with an extraordinary assortment of demotic voices, and by establishing a convincing continuum between the world we ordinarily inhabit and the other world of the work of art.

More Nourishment: Rejoyce

Everything I said above about Keats might also, of course, have come to Durcan (and Kavanagh) from another source, closer to home. For Joyce's *Ulysses* is a book Durcan, like Kavanagh before him, reveres, and it is in *Ulysses* that one could find sources for many of the elements I've been describing. The notion that life is fundamentally good, for example, as well as the notions of negative capability and poetical character are embodied in Leopold Bloom, while the stylistic inhabitation of others — people, things, thoughts, whatever — is what makes the Circe/Nighttown chapter the extraordinary carnival of metamorphoses it is. Aside from these, Joyce's astounding capacity for voice-invention must have left its mark, even if we go no further than the collision between flagrant and fragrant colloquialism to be heard in the movement from the crass narrator of the Cyclops chapter to the genteel tones of Gerty MacDowell in Nausicaa.

Bloom's openness to the other, human and otherwise, is apparent throughout the novel. Whether he is sympathising with 'Poor Mrs Purefoy's' pregnancy ('Sss. Dth, dth, dth!

Three days imagine groaning on a bed with a vinegared handkerchief around her forehead, her belly swollen out! Phew! Dreadful simply!'), wondering about the blind youth's sense of smell, listening to the typesetting machine 'doing its level best to speak', or hearing the creak of a door 'asking to be shut', Bloom is perpetually engaged by the world outside himself. And the simple formulation Joyce gives him in order to reveal this definitive and endearing feature could also apply to Durcan's strategy of multiple voices, rooting it in a particular, and particularly receptive, response to the world: for 'everything', says Bloom, 'speaks in its own way'. Nor is Bloom's perpetual going out from himself, his openness to the polyglottal nature of the world, escapist in the ordinary sense: he does not use it in order to censor his pain about Molly's infidelity, or his aches over his own life, although it can sometimes serve as therapeutic distraction. It is, rather, the action of what Keats called 'the poetical character', while Bloom's almost infinite tolerance — the moral extension of his sympathetic nature — is 'negative capability' in action, standing up against the purveyors of egotistic and nationalistic 'facts and reasons', his whole existence a testament to unirritable persistence in the hard life of uncertainty.

As far as stylistic instruction is concerned, *Ulysses* contains numerous specific elements that likely marked Durcan's work. Chapters such as Cyclops and Nausicaa, as I've said, are treasure troves of speech possibility in their two radically different registers of the colloquial. A random dip into the first produces the following gem of unaffected Dublinese: 'And begob there he was passing the door with his books under his oxter and the wife beside him and Corny Kelleher with his wall eye looking in as they went past, talking to him like a father, trying to sell him a secondhand coffin'.

An equally random encounter with 'Nausicaa' finds this very different sound: 'Gerty MacDowell who was seated near her companions, lost in thought, gazing far away into the distance was in very truth as fair a specimen of winsome Irish girlhood as one could wish to see'. Such influxes of Dublin speech in its different registers into his work (most of his voices, I'd say, have a definite Dublin colour and texture) should remind us that Durcan's own insistence on his Mayo roots need not distract from the fact that he is — along with Clarke, Kinsella and, more recently, Paula Meehan — a quintessentially Dublin poet.

Beyond this stimulus to distinctive speech, *Ulysses* must also have prompted Durcan's natural inclination towards the metamorphic. In the Circe/Nighttown chapter, metamorphosis is everywhere: whether a bar of soap sings or a bicycle bell shrieks, everything not only 'speaks in its own way' but is able at the slightest provocation to turn into something else. A ceaseless, dreamlike fluency of matter and character dissolves all borders, rattles all categories out of themselves, so the certain concrete world becomes infinitely plastic, fluid, uncertain, and the borders dissolve even between such stubbornly separate entities as this life and the next world, or male and female genders. The sheer exuberance and abundance of these transformations have, I imagine, made a deep and deeply creative impression on Durcan, accounting in part not only for the variety of his inventions and the ease with which he adopts male and female voices, but for the amazing fluency of matter within the poems themselves. So Mayo may be seen in the light of Asia Minor, Christ is on the road to Moone, a woman keeps her breasts in the back garden, a father and son get married 'in the church of Crinkle near Birr', a man of forty 'has spent all his life reclining in his wife's lap,/ Being given birth to by her again and again', a daughter daubs slime on the face of her snail father lying 'under the great snail cairn of Newgrange'.

Mimic and metamorphic, therefore, it is easy to see how Joyce's style would be crucial to Durcan's evolution of his own poetic strategies, while the moral nature of Joyce's hero, Bloom, would be equally crucial to the moral configuration Durcan puts on his world. For, in Bloom, Joyce offers an exhilarating mixture of unflinching materialism and utopian idealism, a tolerant nationalism (Bloom insists, in tones very different from the apoplectic MacMorris that Ireland is his country: 'Ireland . . . I was born here, Ireland') married to universal humanism and humane-ism, a condition of rarely achieved balance between understanding and judgement. It is an equilibrium Durcan — in his very different, often hidden way — is after.

Vox Pop & The Meaning of It All

In stringing together these bits and pieces from Keats and Kavanagh and Joyce, my purpose is not to suggest that Durcan is doing the same thing over again, or doing it in their shadow, but that he has in one way or another been nourished by what is implicit and explicit in their work or in their notions of poetry, of the poet. I believe that ideas such as these have been his creative sustenance, that they make possible and sustain his own idiosyncratic art. And when I ask myself what central and more or less general feature of his art is most explicitly owed to these ideas, I keep turning to the concept of *extension*. For what the Keats ideas, the Kavanagh practise, the Joyce style, the Bloom way of the world have in common is a notion of extension. And extension is a defining mark of Durcan's work: whether in the notice he pays to an overlooked detail or in the way he brings normally hidden voices to articulate life, he is always extending our sympathy for the ordinary, the local, the trivial, the mundane.

The possibility of extending consciousness (the poet's version, I suppose, of Stephen Dedalus' ambition to forge in the smithy of his soul the uncreated conscience of his race) may also be what directs Durcan's striking public recitals of his own poems. For in the intense plucking apart of the phonetic components of language that these entail, his voice draws inexorably to our attention the slightest detail of linguistic presence. The smallest trace of *coloratura* in a vowel or a diphthong is heard for itself, as is the decisively aspirated or sibilant finality of a consonant, or the slightest modulation of tone or accent — allowing whole characters, whole forms of life to come alive in slow motion, embodied by his language and its aural resources (for, as he well knows, *everything speaks in its own way*). Such art is surely an art of extension, enlarging our sense both of the world and of the word. It is an art at once meticulous, reassuring, and estranging. Meticulous in the quality of its attention, reassuring in the way it restores what has been overlooked to its properly acknowledged place in the world, and estranging because the quality of the performance makes the language feel odd and unfamiliar to us. While on the page it may seem, for all its strangeness, to be anchored in everyday colloquial usage, in the poet's own inimitable performance it becomes a *ritual* of the colloquial. Beyond its own specific local meanings, then, each poem as performed by the poet has an additional significance, a significance that might be attached to his work as a whole. For in these performances (which carry their own measure of instruction to us as readers, strong hints on how to hear the poems when we read them to ourselves) the ordinary is granted, in an extraordinarily vivid and immediate way, the quality and status of ritual. And finally, in a neat reversal and paradox (forms peculiarly appropriate to the instinctively Christian interior of much of Durcan's work, its weightless migrations through time and space), this act of estrangement is really an instrument of renewed recognition, creating a fresh association and connection with the subject. On the page and in performance Durcan's poems reconnect us with the world, so that in the end connectedness itself is his subject — whether he writes out of his even-handed resistance to public atrocities in Northern Ireland, or out of the divided private region of his broken marriage, fractured family life, the aching gap between father and son. With connectedness as its implicit theme, his work extends our sense of the world, just as his own connection to Joyce and Kavanagh allows him to extend his creative world, and by doing so to establish a body of poetry that has become central to contemporary Irish art and, in turn, contemporary Irish consciousness. In his work, that is, he extends what we might call our tradition, and by doing so, extends, in his own remarkable way, us all.

Soul Music

Thinking about her own belief in God and in certain acts of religious piety, Molly Bloom presumes that her husband would 'scoff if he heard because he never goes to church mass or meeting he says your soul you have no soul inside only grey matter because he doesn't know what it is to have one.' Unlike Leopold Bloom (whatever about Joyce), Durcan seems to have what we might call belief in 'the soul'. Belief, in fact, whether its status be theological or otherwise, is a mark of his stance towards experience and the world from early on. As he says in 'The Butterfly is the Hardest Stroke',

I have not "met" God, I have not "read"
David Gascoyne, James Joyce, or Patrick Kavanagh:
I believe in them.

It is this quality of belief that lends its peculiar touch of authenticity to Durcan's best work. Whether located in a region of conventional belief (such as the church in '10.30 a.m. Mass, 16 June 1985' — Bloomsday! — or 'The Crucifixion Circus, Good Friday, Paris, 1981') or in a sexually animated but guiltless environment conventionally at odds with (Irish) religion ('Teresa's Bar', for example, or the bedrooms in 'Phyllis Goldberg', 'Lifesaving', or the erotic kitchen in 'Around the Corner from Francis Bacon'), a great number of the best poems testify to an affirmative faith in that 'fundamental goodness' of life which he learned from Kavanagh, a faith to which he, like Kavanagh, often gives a 'feminine' character. In terms of style, too — in the way the poems embrace the language and what might be called its sacramental possibility (using its ordinary resources to reveal an extraordinary world) — Durcan at his best communicates belief in what he is saying, and the intensity of faith gives buoyancy as well as conviction to his lines, no matter how weird or unlikely their contents. Whereas the work of Derek Mahon might be described as a poetry of profound scepticism shot through with thin and intermittent flickers of belief, and the work of Seamus Heaney might be seen as a poetry of belief tempered by a stubbornly sceptical naturalism, the work of Durcan seems to live in an unqualified region of faith. But not of transcendence. The faith is comic, self-aware, human, irrational, a blithe transgressive mix of the here and there, the then and now. It is a faith, too, that trusts itself sufficiently to make mistakes, to take risks, to sound silly. Finally, it is a faith that finds characteristic serio-comic expression in one of his most recent and, it seems to me, best pieces, 'A Spin in the

Rain with Seamus Heaney'. 'I have always thought', he remarks, as he and Heaney play a desultory game of ping-pong, 'that ping-pong balls — / Static spheres fleet as thoughts — / Have flight textures similar to souls.' Surprising as this association is, it is no surprise that it leads to a connection between soul and poetry. For isn't that what it's all been leading to, and what even these comments of mine have been leading up to? Certainly it is what this poem comes to rest in, ending as it does with Durcan's withdrawal into the place where soul and poetry intersect, the musical space where poetry becomes not only an expression of the spirit, but a moral agent:

> *As darkness drops, the rain clears.*
> *I take leave of you to prepare my soul*
> *For tonight's public recital. Wishing each other well.*
>
> *Poetry! To be able to look a bullet in the eye,*
> *With a whiff of the bat to return it spinning to drop*
> *Down scarcely over the lapped net; to stand still; to*
> *stop.*

Your Daddy, My Daddy

Peggy O'Brien

This essay is personal, which is not to say that it will be unduly emotional: only that it comes out of a question long held personally, one that is rooted in my individual situation. I am an American woman living and writing in the United States, but I lived for most of my adult life in Ireland. My sympathies and insights and most of my reading flow in two directions, which is why I have wondered for a long time about Paul Durcan's choice of title, *Daddy, Daddy* for one of his best collections of poetry. "Daddy, Daddy" is perhaps the single most resonant phrase in the canon of women's poetry. What is the dialogue Durcan is having with Sylvia Plath, the author of the original phrase from the poem 'Daddy' in *Ariel*, and what does his choice of title signify as a moment in cultural history?

Maybe my fascination is grounded in envy or simple wonder. No American male or female could do such a thing. A man would never dare, knowing the charges of heinous appropriation, vile presumption that would await him. How, I ask myself, does Durcan as a man feel immune to the accusations? Does being an Irish male, an heir to the legacy of feminization and victimization under colonialism, provide him with an exemption? For any woman, come to think of it, of any nationality to use the title would be interpreted as either slavish imitation or usurpation, pretending to the throne, pathetic either way.

Plath's ground-breaking concluding line to 'Daddy', a ringing declaration, 'Daddy, daddy, you bastard, I'm through', is by now a landmark in women's poetry. It has the inviolable singularity as a moment in cultural history that Patrick Kavanagh's oracular opening to the 'The Great Hunger' has for Irish poets, particularly men: 'Clay is the word and clay is the flesh'. Both moments are epiphanies in the long, collective search for a voice. Nothing is the same afterwards. Both represent the arrival at a confidence great enough to speak a revealed truth, to know and say something that was unthinkable before. Their sacredness derives precisely from their courting of heresy, overturning previously accepted pieties concerning the docility and servility of peasants and women. Both install their heresies as new doctrines, bestow on them that degree of authority.

Such moments of revelation and articulation are not repeatable. They 'occur', as Wallace Staves would put it, 'as they occur', convergences of temperament and history and talent. To repeat or echo these moments silently, or even in conversation, is natural enough, like invoking a prayer. But to repeat them deliberately and commit them to print is another matter entirely and needs justification. Furthermore, to parody these lines is to dare to make history oneself, lay down another layer of culture.

With Durcan I believe the repetition is not even as inadvertently patronizing as simple homage. It's profound identification on many levels, levels that must interest the cultural historian. Durcan's sequence of poems, 'Daddy, Daddy', which gives the title to the collection in which it appears, marks a rare moment in the intricate story of literary influence, a moment that muddies the pristine model Harold Bloom via Freud created in *The Anxiety of Influence* to describe such relationships. Bloom essentially assigned strong poets the role of unconsciously misreading previous strong poets — precursors, males, fathers — out of the necessity to make room for themselves. Breaking with Bloom's prognosis, I believe that Plath is both a profound influence on Durcan and one of whom he is conscious, that the title *Daddy, Daddy* is a tuning fork of intertextuality and that the echoes of *Ariel* are too audible within Durcan to be unwitting. They are definite signals sent by the literate author to the literate reader. Durcan may not be conscious of the full extent of the influence, but that is less important than his admission in the title. Very much in keeping with Bloom, however, the swerve Durcan makes away from Plath is his defining signature. Where Durcan's behavior fundamentally breaks with Bloom's paradigm is in allowing himself to embrace a woman's words so intimately, to let them seep so far down into his imagination. It is a psychologically shrewd and complicated move on Durcan's part to allow a woman's influence to inform the poetic that determines a poem centered on a Oedipal conflict. This is not a move predicted by Bloom.

I would like to trace here, very lightly and briefly, both the blatant echoes and deeper thematic and stylistic resemblances, above all the shared and unshared ontological problems evident in both the sequence 'Daddy, Daddy' and Plath's *Ariel*. Finally I want to sketch the path of Durcan's divergence from Plath, how this deviance defines both her uniqueness and his.

When you start looking for them, the echoes seem endless, starting on the most visible level of image. 'You do not do, you do not do/ Any more, black shoe.' So begins Plath's

'Daddy'. Durcan gives over an entire poem, 'Bare Feet', to the image of black shoes:

> *'When I was forty-three years old,*
> *In the year of your dying,*
> *And I needed a new pair of shoes*
> *You offered me an old pair of your own shoes,*
> *Stately big black men o' war*
> *With long, thin, twiney black laces.'*

The martial air is pure Plath but Durcan's shoes are more detailed, the features of their forbidding but finally quirky physiognomies filled in. The little comic touch, those 'long, thin, twiney black laces', is part of the big difference. Such separating happens, however, in dynamic, dialectical intimacy with Plath, sometimes seeming to clone her. Those very specific and individual forty-three years collapse into Plath's by now canonic 'thirty years' in the poem by Durcan that directly precedes 'Bare Feet'. 'Geronimo' begins, 'Although we were estranged lovers/ For almost thirty years.'

This unseemly fusion of father and son, caricatured as marriage, reinscribes Plath's double conflation of her father with her husband and of both with her. Packaged as one, the two men, unreliable sources of life, must be done without, the cord cut: 'The black telephone's off at the root,/ The voices just can't worm through' ('Daddy'). Plath's father's voice, the memory of him that worms through her mind, is always black and dank and subterranean, lethal, the grave. A similar iconography appears in Durcan's 'Stellar Manipulator': 'Seven a.m. on a black Sunday morning/ In Ladbroke Grove./ The black telephone. Your black voice.' The difference in the Durcan poem is that the saturnine father comes to London, puts up bail for his errant son, gives him a fresh start.

Judge Durcan, however, appears throughout the early poems as a fascist and remains fixed as this until the son's perspective on the father and himself becomes more accepting, flexible. The sequence derives much of its emotional force from charting this gradual melting, which has not begun in 'Mother's Boy', a poem about a father-son jaunt out into the Dublin mountains, an excursion into enforced closeness that results in pronounced emotional distance:

I contemplate the cut of your jib
Through buttercup and fern,
Your resemblance to Mussolini
Mussolini topping his egg.

Even here a trickle of humour (that bald egg being topped) dilutes a potentially corrosive hate.

In Plath, however, because anger goes unchecked, is reveled in as tangible and free-flowing at last, blood gushing from her thumb in 'Cut', this anger eats into the reader's mind like acid. Her lines are indelible. For better or worse 'Every woman adores a fascist' has become received doctrine rather than subjective observation. Despite the man-hating and self-loathing heart of *Ariel*, Durcan keeps registering his affinities with it through an extended iteration of its imagery. Plath in 'Daddy' turns her father into 'not God but a swastika/ So black no sky could squeak through'. Durcan ascribes a not unrelated, airtight moral evasiveness to his father in the remarkable poem, 'Fjord', which beyond its personal content carries implications about Irish history, specifically Ireland's stance of putative neutrality during World War II. The poem ends: 'Look into your Irish heart, you will find a German U-boat,/ A periscope in the rain and a swastika in the sky.'

The most stunning, almost outlandishly faithful repetition, occurs between an early poem in *Ariel* and a late poem in 'Daddy, Daddy'. Again, so many lines in Plath resonate with history that they cannot be echoed without the echo itself making history. Plath's 'Tulips' begins, 'The tulips are too excitable, it is winter here.' In 'Our Father', a sweet-tempered, leisurely poem, the last in fact in 'Daddy, Daddy', Durcan very obviously rewrites a Plath line. Since the title of the poem is parodic and the text even includes portions of the best known of Christian prayers, an invocation to God the Father, it seems reasonable to assume that parody in this instance extends to Plath. Here Durcan is deliberately and ostentatiously veering away from Plath's relationship with her Daddy. Durcan's lines, spoken by a bus conductor with a gardening fetish, read: 'My grapes, for example, Grapes are too excitable.' But Durcan's comical floramaniac goes on and on:

I have to keep each grape separate from the other.
Time-consuming it is
Keeping all my grapes separate from each other.
Each grape has to be totally separate from the next
  grape.

The irony is that both the poet passenger and the bus conductor are excitable but are having an exciting, unconventionally intimate encounter. The mood is celebratory, life affirming. Their conversation, more a monologue by the conductor, begins by his admiring the bouquet of irises the poet is bringing to his mother, per his father's order in 'Geronimo' long before his death. 'Our Father' is a poem about the stubborn and beautiful persistence of life, registered most by the receptivity of the poet to the conductor, donating the voice of the poem to him, someone who simply refuses, unlike Plath, to live in winter, who dwells in the greenhouse of his dreams, full of color and warmth and freedom. He refuses on this occasion even to collect fares from the other passengers. Some moments, whole days, must be free of charge, since others cost so dearly, like the moment of death.

Ariel is an unrelenting work; there are no such respites. In 'Tulips' the poet patient, who has been sent the offending blooms in hospital, centers her energy on resisting their seduction, the expensive vibrancy they exude, the cost of all feeling, all living beyond the white walls of affective numbness. The only desire in the poem can seem to be to have no desire, to discover the Zen perfection of emptiness, 'to lie with my hands turned up and be utterly empty.' This poem with its iambic pentameter lines, relatively long for the breathlessly paced *Ariel*, and with its seven-line stanzas shaped like successive points in an argument, is ironically a wordy defense of not caring. It manages to communicate *sotto voce*, in counterpoint, a desire finally to be understood. At the same time, an undertow of black silence threatens all the way through to draw the very ink of the words down through the white funnel of the poet's papery skin, drained of the blood of desire, into peacefulness, aloneness at last. Nothing could be more in contrast with the jostle and crack on Durcan's No. 14 bus to Dartry (Not the No. 13 to Palmerston Park, mind, where life being life, such a marvellous, serendipitous encounter might not have happened.)

So why the uncanny resemblances and the firm differences? Obviously this is not a case of slavish imitation or gross indebtedness but of deeply empathic connection on one poet's part with another perceived to be wrestling with familiar formal and psychological problems. The astonishing breakthrough that *Ariel* represents for Plath, a stylistic and personal liberation that finds its resounding, apocalyptic proclamation in 'Daddy', is its chief attraction, I believe, for Durcan. The wresting of a totally natural idiom and the taking of bold risks with rhythm and line structure make *Ariel* revolutionary in the context of Plath's hitherto more cautious oeuvre. Just the unselfconsciousness to sound like an American finally, to know she can use slang and lose not a single degree of seriousness, indeed increase it by the sound of unleashed rage, marks her poetic maturity. 'Lady Lazarus' would not have half its power if Plath couldn't swagger in pure American, 'Dying/ Is an art, like everything else./ I do it exceptionally well./ I do it so it feels like hell' and brag of her survival after a suicide attempt, calling it 'A miracle!'/ That knocks me out.' Any Irish poet, like Plath (not only an American but an American living in England and married to an English poet), is going to be constantly aware, if only in the corner of his eye, of the august profile of the English poetic tradition. An Irish writer with a temperament as iconoclastic as Durcan's is bound to be stirred by the spectacle of Plath throwing off the manacles of conventions no longer useful for her voice.

The most intense and intensely vocal poems in *Ariel*, however, its famous, by now infamous dramatic monologues, like 'Lady Lazarus', 'Daddy', 'The Applicant' and 'Fever 103°', represent only a handful of the poems in the collection, the majority of which are less febrile, quieter, if possible darker. Anger buoys the monologues which demand rather than court a listener. The more meditative poems delve deeper than the anger, plumb despair, fatal ambiguities of identity. It is these poems that provide the most telling clues to Plath's and, by way of comparison, Durcan's poetics. After all, Durcan already possesses a visceral, spontaneous voice long before *Daddy, Daddy*. In that book he weds his deceptively nonchalant, transparent speech with material of such psychological complexity that the apparent insouciance on the surface of the poems stands in arresting tension with their sinister depths. It is this tightrope act, patented by Plath, that Durcan emulates.

For both writers confronting the Father is one of the most daring acts they can perform. Both books are courageous investigations of identity through the paternal line. Plath confesses to her search in 'Daddy':

I used to pray to recover you.
Ach, du.
In the German tongue, in the Polish town
...But the name of the town is common.

The crucial aspect of this search for origin, finding the one, precise town, is its coincidence with a search for authentic language, truly the *mot juste*. Plath ends her stanza with a confession finally to muteness: 'I never could talk to you./ The tongue stuck in my jaw.'

Durcan brings the same two necessities together in relation to his father. For Durcan, the Dubliner, being able to root the father in the West of Ireland provides relief. It assigns a source for father and son both in the soil rather than the ether of the law, a supererogatory reminder of the father's stern Oedipal presence, enforcing even the hint of a taboo. One of Durcan's most restrained, quietly elegiac poems in the collection, 'The One Armed Crucifixion', glows with the warmth of a genuinely shared experience playing hurling 'on the shore at Galway', the rhyme of '*sliotar*' and 'other' bonding the two and beyond that bonding the father to a particular, indigenous culture. The poem concludes by delicately asserting the son's achievement of separation in an image of self-mastery, despite the self-effacement in the concluding question mark: 'To crouch, to dart, to leap/ To pluck the ball one-handed out of the climbing air?' That one-handed catch is Durcan's deft escape from symbiosis. The beauty of the image, a poetic rather than athletic achievement, predicts the son's eventual consolidation of this separateness through his own poetry. Part of the compelling drama of 'Daddy, Daddy' is watching the parallel developments in different directions of a father dying and a son growing in strength as a poet by depicting the double process. It is an enactment rather than an ironic, retrospective narration of a portrait of an artist.

The poem of Durcan's that most completely explores the double question of identity and language as received from the father is 'The Mayo Accent'. In the first stanza, showing rather than telling through lush, exotic images, the poem records the loss involved in the father's betrayal of his natural accent:

Have you ever tuned in to the voice of a Mayoman?
In his mouth the English language is sphagnum moss
Under the bare braceleted feet of a pirate queen.

What is more, this is not language abandoned to the anarchy of nature unruled by law, the equivalent of emotion denied the containments poetry offers, rather this is nature tempered gently but firmly by natural law, ancient and irrefutable:

Speech in Mayo is a turbary function
To be exercised as a turbary right
With turbary responsibilities
Peatsmoke of silence unfurls over turf fires of language.

The tradition-bound parceling out of the bog, assigning boundaries and rights, is both imperative and implicit, the way a silence at the heart of an ellipsis reigns without question.

Durcan's father exchanged this gracious, natural speech for the prim elocutions of the bench and acquired the starchy accent to go with them:

Why then, Daddy, did you shed
The pricey antlers of your Mayo accent
For the tree-felling voice of a harsh judiciary
Whose secret headquarters were in the Home Counties
    or High Germany?

The son's project is to understand the father's impurities, to avoid the irony of being a harsh judge himself.

Durcan's view of his father will moderate, soften, but not until he has exhausted the conceit of seeing the father as a fascist, a Nazi, and understood more completely the causes which underlie this dictatorial posture. Comedy, however, perpetually propels and refreshes Durcan in his drive to understand. He remarks in flashback in a later, more mellow poem, 'The Dream in a Peasant's Bent Shoulders', that the only vacation on which Daddy ever took his wife was 'A pilgrimage by coach to the home of Mussolini.' The poems that operate most as exorcisms of Daddy's evil influence are those that draw most heavily on the rhetorical devices of Plath's incandescent monologues, chiefly her use of repetition. Whereas Plath mainly wields triads ('at twenty I tried to die/ And get back, back, back to you' from 'Daddy'; 'adhering to rules, to rules, to rules,' from 'A Birthday Present'; 'These are the isolate, slow faults/ That kill, that kill, that kill,' from 'Elm'), Durcan, who makes a fetish of excess, repeats and repeats and repeats. He gives the poem the chance to become a process, to evolve rather than dramatise a single, immutable, rigid stance. In 'Figure in a Landscape, 1952', for example, fear has the time to become confusion, somersault into relief and end up unexpectedly as blind, stock-still terror. The poem, a dialogue, enacts a mock interrogation conducted under the merciless glare of the judge and concerns the crucial question of bodily elimination. It becomes, through the sheer degree of repetition in which it indulges, an exploration of the absurd. The word 'Bowels' is repeated ten times, the meek reply 'Daddy' thirty-one times. Finally, when the father pronounces pompously on his philosophy of evacuation — 'Constipation is the curse of Cain/ ...If your bowels do not move, you are doomed' — the reader understands, if the trembling little boy still does not, that the father is blocked in more subtle ways than rectally, that repression reaches up far into consciousness and beyond into the unconscious, making free and easy speech along with free and easy social intercourse almost impossible.

It is only when the child admits to messy confusion that the anal retentiveness of the father which has dominated the situation relaxes. The child is forced to admit that he doesn't know what bowels are, that he thinks 'bowels are wheels/ ....black wheels under my tummy'. At this precise moment the child unwittingly discovers, though the irony is deliberate on the poet's part, what will be his salvation. The basic confusion of one thing with another can become metaphor, poetry: purity will not be Durcan's way. No sooner does the child admit to his ignorance, no sooner is this moment of play and humor and fruitful chaos passed through, that movement on the literal level of the poem occurs: ' I want to go to the toilet, Daddy.' Daddy's control, however, overpowers even this moment of limited autonomy over the body as the father imposes a race on the child with his own bowels. The strain of competition gives way to a terror of failure and punishment: 'Don't, Daddy, don't, Daddy, don't Daddy, don't.'

The other poem in the Durcan sequence where repetition is the dominant rhetorical strategy, 'Dovecote', links the father's neuroses with the trauma of a nation and the word that forms a refrain is 'Eviction', becoming at the end the imperative, '*Evict*'. The concluding triad is Plathian, the very last line with its faint echo of the end of 'Lady Lazarus' — 'I eat men like air' — as close as Durcan comes in these poems to glimpsing the white, nihilistic light that eerily illuminates *Ariel*. For Durcan the remembered holocaust is the Great Famine and its legacy of spiritual impoverishment his theme: '*Evict*: Why do priests eat gods?/ *Evict*: Why do gentlemen commit suicide?/ *Evict*: Do doves eat doves? Souls souls?' The solipsism implied by one abstraction swallowing another represents the most extreme point that the poem and the sequence reach in pure abstraction.

For Plath the insistence on abstract evil is unrelieved. Her father's demonic appearance merges with that of her husband, 'A man in black with a Meinkampf look' ('Daddy'). So powerful is the terror inspired by this visage that mute autism is the response: 'Ich, ich, ich, ich', those four fricatives being the chaos that precedes vicious articulation. The poet's voice is dependent paradoxically on the ever-present threat of complete annulment that the father's remembered, censoring presence imposes. Speech, like living through a suicide attempt, is a matter of constantly defying the odds. The plain speech of *Ariel* is the result of finally effectively combating the 'gobbledygoo' of the 'Panzer-man'. Such self-generated speech involves a violent throwing off of every vestige of the father's Aryan standards, all he tried to teach and instill, hence the looser language and the arrogation to herself of the sensuality she projects onto Jewishness, an act of the imagination parallel to Durcan's identification with a woman, a victim, and a poet.

Plath reminds the reader that her tyrannical father was a pedagogue: 'You stand at the blackboard, daddy, in the picture I have of you' ('Daddy'). Durcan represents his father as essentially a teacher, reminding the judge in 'Fjord': 'You were a teacher before you were a judge.' Again the pedagogue's words are 'gobbledygoo': '"*Fjord*" — you'd announce — "is a Norwegian word."' These two northern, icy, exacting fathers, keeping their own counsel as they keep their uncertainty and emotions well hidden, leave their excessively loving, sensitive, needy offspring imagining the awful emotional content behind the blank facade, inhabiting this sealed-off hell themselves. Red is the color in Plath of emergence up and through the white anger that embalms her, making her dead to herself and unnaturally at one with her dead father. In 'Lady Lazarus' she finds the temerity to rise fueled by the acetylene energy of poetry and become herself a cannibal, as terrifying to others as a tulip once was to her. Like the 'Poppies in July' she becomes fire, 'Little poppies, little hell fires.'

Fire as apocalypse figures in 'Daddy, Daddy' and equally connects with the central effort of finding words as a way to climb out of the unspoken anger always threatening to explode into incendiary catastrophe. Durcan being Durcan, however, every allusion to this hallucinatory level of the family nightmare, ultimately his bout with depression, as it was for Plath, is laced with humor. In 'Crinkle, near Birr', where father and son go on holiday, a second honeymoon to reunite as a couple after years of estrangement, the son now has the droll distance from his father to quip: 'Daddy divided the human race/ Into those who had fire escapes and spoke Irish/ And those who had not got fire escapes and did not speak Irish,' a metaphoric way on Durcan's part of describing someone disarmingly punitive and elusive.

In the preceding poem in the sequence, 'The Persian Gulf', placed in a much earlier time, when the poet is a child, there is not the same detached understanding. The child fails to see the anxiety that eats away at the tyrant and the remoteness that results from denial of this fear. Through the apocalyptic fantasy that figures in 'The Persian Gulf', a conflagration that leaves the family escaping through a skylight in the roof of their bourgeois, Dartmouth Square house, Durcan revisits the scene of 'Six Nuns Die in Convent Inferno' and turns it into black comedy. The later poem begins, 'The skylight is our escape route in the event of fire'. It is no coincidence that this is the same aperture through which the twelve-year-old boy glimpses his parents in a primal act. In 'The Persian Gulf' the entire family is reciting the rosary in Irish and to the young poet the circular exercise becomes 'the great Ferris wheel of the Rosary', each prayer in enforced Irish the occasion for a flare-up of resentment:

I dream of the Persian Gulf and try
To imagine what the skylight would look like
On fire but I can no more visualise it
Than I can visualise the prayers we are saying
In a language in which we do not converse
And which is as strange to me as French or German
Praying in Irish to a skylight is an abstract art.

In the last line Durcan is coming close to the heart of his poetic. His art is earthed, though from its vantage point we often receive an unplanned metaphysical glimpse, like a comet passing.

Durcan's career could be persuasively summarised as a sustained effort to practice what is not an abstract art. In the poem 'Lifesaving', where the parents are glimpsed having sex, the father's disingenuous answer to the son's genuine question of what was happening is, 'Your mother was teaching me lifesaving.' Avoiding unnecessary, merely self-punishing abstraction, practicing a love of the actual world, is life saving, sanity preserving for the poet. The most memorable moments in a Durcan poem frequently occur when, casually, without any rule or program, he allows into his ken a heartbreaking, marginal detail of life. The mere inclusion of urban flotsam in a Durcan poem can draw the reader instantly into the orbit of a life lived unself-consciously, well beyond the reach of over-determining imagination, as dangerous as an over-controlling father.

One such sublimely quotidian moment occurs in 'Exterior with Plant, Reflection Listening' where Durcan, standing at a bus stop, gives us this: ' The boy sitting beside a pram of apples/ Has his arms folded, thinking of something else.' The poet even notices that the boy has had his hair permed. In 'Glocca Morra' at his father's death-bed Durcan observes 'paintwork flaking on the wall' and notes a transistor radio in the background playing that old Rosemary Clooney tune with the comically abstract title about a make-believe, vaguely Celtic place where people don't die particular, demeaning deaths.

This gravitation toward random fact, the ordinary unmediated by romantic imagination, seems in Durcan a direct reaction against a period of confusion, when fact and fantasy collapsed. These moments too, however, are revisited by imagination and converted to comic surrealism: an alligator sighted in the bathtub of blood-thirsty, tabloid-consuming British suburbanites, Cliff and Cheryl in '1966', who play for an entire, grotesque afternoon The Eve of Destruction, the broken record of their boring, insufficiently mad lives. Pushing against the hermeticism of the nuclear family, always in danger of becoming radioactive,

Durcan moves out into the world, the city, breathing in its Brueghelesque variety. With wry control, however, he can still savor the mind's wondrous slippages, like sitting in the Kentucky Grill, absentmindedly eating and remembering in his grief his deceased father: 'When Daddy died I gazed upon his chips — / I mean, his features.' Metonymy can be a useful means of staying sane.

Durcan in the sequence makes through his lengthy argument with his father a poetic grounded in specifics, in flux, in salutary hybridity. For all his nostalgia about the essentialist West, he is most at home in the tackily hybrid Kentucky Grill in O'Connell St. Rage at the father's holier-than-thou espousal of Irish crossed on the hypocrisy of devotion to golf, cricket and rugby, those most English of pastimes, becomes in the end a rich appreciation of a unique character. Idiosyncrasies align themselves into the detailed portrait of a real man, neither an icon nor a demon. The sequence allows us to witness first-hand the dialectical process by which this balanced view develops.

Durcan's poetic characteristically alternates between detached, static moments often bounded by a trope, moments equivalent to the photograph snapped in 'Geronimo' ('He sat in profile/ While I crouched behind a holly tree/ Snapping him with my Japanese camera') and long, long stretches of story. In storytelling mode Durcan affords himself the latitude of digression and the deceptive ease of lifelike speech. His world becomes capacious, big enough for anything and everything, a Japanese camera taking a photograph of an Irish-speaking judge who has become a true hybrid: 'Old Bare Feet/ And Indian elder tinker man' ('Bare Feet').

By the end of 'Daddy, Daddy', the father, targeted by death, is the stigmatised other, not the son who in his early, unstable years, before voice saved him, identified with all forms of branded otherness. At a rugby match between Ireland and South Africa, shortly after his release from a mental hospital, the young poet imagines himself as the black man (the black sheep) nowhere in evidence on the field, essentially the father's limited field of vision. The poem 'Apartheid' makes it clear how much the atmosphere of oppression is connected with language, the absolute dominance of the father's voice:

> *He pronounces the word 'Apartheid'*
> *With such élan, such expertise,*
> *With such familiarity, such finality*
> *As if it were a part of nature,*
> *Part of ourselves.*

The poet's maturing demands recreating a world through the logos of his own speech, as dictated by his own nature.

The rhythm of these poems, expanding out into detail and story and contracting back into accessible, loosely constructed trope, is the natural rhythm of a mind conversing with itself and the world by turns. It is, for example, Whitman's chosen mode of operation, establishing the rhythm of breathing, inhalation, exhalation, as the template for the poetic line. The body becomes the palimpsest for the poem. One of the most perfectly constructed and moving poems in the Durcan sequence, 'Antwerp, 1984', uses this Whitmanesque method to determine its structure, weaving into dilatory conversation, mimetic of a train's progress, poignant snapshots, literally reflections in a train window of an old man with Parkinson's disease and a son absorbed by his own worry and needs. At one point, reflection brings the two temporarily together: 'Our eyes meet, each of us/ yearning for what the other yearns.' Reflection, poetry, becomes a helpful mediator, an aid to empathy and a useful barrier to pathological fusion of identities.

In 'Geronimo' this mature closeness that includes separateness takes the form of a continuous story told in turns. The story, about Pearse's visit to Corkery's house, has been told many times by them to each other. Father and son both know the script and their separate parts. The father's customary line is to identify the novel associated with the house where Pearse stayed, *The Threshold of Quiet*. With a whisper of metaphor the poet identifies for the reader the threshold over which the father imminently will pass.

The sequence as a whole becomes on one level the story of one man's gradual dying, a remarkably quiet process, not a single calamitous event. It's even more the story of a relationship which is equally a process, full of incident, conflict, moods, resolutions and new problems. Nothing is static, most of all anger and this is true even at the grim beginning. During the eidetic crisis in 'The Persian Gulf', when the family is stranded among flames on the rooftop and the father rejects help from the non-Irish speaking fireman, we know they will all be saved by the proto-poet who quenches the flames with his comic sensibility. Hilarity puts out the fire of his panic: 'Daddy stands by a chimney pot, admiring the night sky, / Looking like Danny Kaye in *The Court Jester*'.

In part the detachment eventually and fully gained is the straightforward result of negotiating an old-fashioned Oedipal crisis. We know by 'Susannah and the Elders' that the tables are finally turned. The still lecherous father has to be warned by the son that his wife is out-of-bounds. Ironically, it is the laying down of law that puts the son on equal footing with the judge. The resolution of conflict that makes 'Daddy,

Daddy' in the end an unusually tender testimony of filial attachment is due largely to the passage of time, the temporality on which narrative thrives, which it requires. Story must become the backbone of Durcan's poetic because it is the spine too of his identity. It is as though in deference to, or in an effort to stay reconnected with, the real Irishness of his father's storytelling genius (rather than in his stiff loyalty to the Irish language), that Durcan gives orality such a prominent place in his poetic. The form that results is in itself a hybrid, partaking both of the standard conventions of poetry and those of story, a true post-colonial product. Such a mongrel form is an appropriate reflection of the self Durcan comes to accept through the father's dying, someone both himself and his father.

Father and son together tell the story of 'Daddy, Daddy'. The voice Durcan discovers finally is polyglot, indebted to many sources, one prominently other than himself, his father. This is never more apparent than in the poem 'The French Revolution' where at his father's death-bed the son remembers and retells silently in his mind the judge's skewed, potted, rote rendition of the derring-do of Danton and Robespierre. The poet looks back longingly on an innocent time, 'When your children were small,/ Before they got beyond the range of your storytelling/ Before they got lost in a world with no story.' The world without story is the world of fragmented, atomistic images, the world of nightmare or mental illness, where a linking narrative that makes sense of life is missing. By telling the story of his father's death Durcan is restoring the protection of the father to himself, consciously deciding as an adult to live within the consoling circumference of story, fictions. Taking over the patriarchal function of telling the stories means being free to acknowledge indebtedness to the father: 'You were the artist of artists,/ ...Storyteller of storytellers,/ ...Poet of poets'('Chips'). Giving a book of his a title taken from Plath is a similarly grown-up gesture of generosity, an implicit recognition.

The acknowledgement is made easier by the fact that Plath is engaged in a very different project, one determined by a different culture, a different gender, a different personal history. The premature death of her father makes the gradual working out of a relationship impossible. The father is idealised, demonised, arrested, suspended in the mind. He is best approached obliquely through the static, intricate design a difficult trope makes. Plath's poetry is infinitely more knotted, even in the unfettered, swinging rhythms of *Ariel* than Durcan's ever is. Hers is a poetry that trades in absolutes. No compromises are acceptable. Each poem is a duel to the death. As 'Death & Co.' puts it in the last line, 'Somebody's done for.' The necessity for such mutual exclusivity is the much more precarious footing her identity has in a world where abstraction is rarely relieved except by the mitigated sensuality of figure, her extraordinary metaphors, the balloons of the mind that fill up an otherwise barren space. In the poem 'Balloons' the gorgeous 'oval soul-animals' are the only objects in stripped-down rooms, without even furniture. Like her poems they are 'globes of thin air, red, green,/ Delighting/ ...the heart like wishes.' In the first poem in the collection, 'Morning Song,' a baby's cry is a 'handful of notes;/ The clear vowels rise like balloons.' In 'Fever 103°' the poet reports blithely: 'I think I am going up/ I think I may rise' and objectifies herself as:

a lantern —
...My head a moon
Of Japanese paper, my gold beaten skin
Infinitely delicate and infinitely expensive.

These are poems where language is as fine and burnished as the boundary between inspiration and infinity. Each poem has as precarious a life as a balloon, which, when it breaks, leaves the perplexed child confronting the near absolute of pure space, 'contemplating a world clear as water/ A red/ Shred in his little fist.' Notice, however, the way the simile, clear as water, retains for the poet's mind a thin corporeal skin. One of the main and most mysterious reasons for the force of Plath's poetic is the way it hinges on the paradox of imagination finding the possibility of its own absence almost more compelling than its capacity to create.

The fear and the attraction of vanishing into the idea of nothingness is the motivation behind the creation of poems, which are both clear windows onto emptiness and splashes of brilliant, life-preserving colour. Opposite desires are served simultaneously. Durcan's poetic is less a paradox than an achieved synthesis that does not exclude the idea of compromise. For him the poet is 'neither/ Spiritual or animal,/ On average a bit of both/ In a gray/ self-indulgent way' ('Mother's Boy'). For Plath there is no gray. The moral drama is intense. The father remains a Nazi, she a victim, unless the exact opposite pertains, as in 'Stings', where she becomes the God who determines the fate of her bees. She can provide or withhold sustenance, decide whether they live or die, experience the power of her father. Hers is a black-and-white world and the poems rather than containing alternating modes within themselves vacillate, like dual personalities, between more introspective lyrics and extrovert tirades, both strung tightly on paradox. In her highly figured meditations, empty space almost overpowers content, as the oblique angle between vehicle and tenor leaves huge shards of emptiness before the reader's eyes. The beautiful threat of personal annihilation in the book balances overall with extravagant displays of rage. In her harangues the words spurt like a long buried vein of grief for her father freshly opened by the loss of her husband; but the vivid outpouring of anger is always in danger of disappearing underground again, buried alive by forces stronger than language, those 'fixed stars' ('Words') of destiny that have a life independent of mimesis. The fear is always that words anyway will not be received, heard, that the dead father is above all a deaf father: 'Deafness is something else./ Such a dark funnel, my father!' ('Little Fugue').

There is the further fear that authorship is only erratically, inconsistently wrested from a more powerful force: 'I am your opus' ('Lady Lazarus'). The woman becomes the desired, fantasised image in the Cyclopian eye of another creator, a father, a poet-husband. She becomes some man's ultimate poem, his surpassing work of art in the flesh. In 'The Applicant' one of the qualities cited to sell the woman to the man is an obligingness in her that extends to being the protean product of any desire: 'You have an eye, it's an image.' Endless, pliant accommodation means being the reflection of someone else's imagination, becoming loathsome like the moon in 'The Rival', one of the 'great light borrowers'. In her assertive, bitter poems, Plath tears herself violently apart from the metallic coldness of the mirror, but at a price: aloneness and the loss finally of the mirror, poetry itself.

As a woman Plath's experience entails radical differences from Durcan's. It's not just that separation from the mother, so much a matter of mirrors, is different for a woman than a man and may be responsible for Plath's ambivalence about all instances of reflection. Even more essentially, the experience of motherhood includes an evaporation of ego boundaries that threatens the most basic sense of self.

Durcan's work naturally, because of his gender, contains no hint of this ontological ambiguity, epitomised for Plath by pregnancy, the corporeal demonstration of irreducible ambiguity. Motherhood alone can account both for the omnipresent blood in *Ariel* and the ichor of abstraction. Many of the metaphors in the collection defy rational explanation the way a pregnant woman's compound identity defies categorizing into separate, autonomous beings. Plath is communicating the resemblance between metaphor and pregnancy and the accidental, ephemeral nature of both in these cryptic lines from 'Morning Song': 'I'm no more your mother/ Than the cloud that distills a mirror to reflect its own slow/ Effacement at the wind's hand.'

Plath is living in *Ariel* in a rarefied state-of-mind where every poem is the shadow of a cloud over her own body, proving that it's still alive, separate. This is not the terra firma of story, however fanciful, however free. These poems are the last moments of a body about to transcend itself, to become soul, language passing into silence. They live for an ultimately deathly purity. These are poems that remain airborne only by killing, burning like helium everything which is not them. They apotheosize themselves by demonizing the other:

There's a stake in your flat, black heart
And the villagers never liked you.
They are dancing and stamping on you.
They always knew it was you.
Daddy, Daddy, you bastard, I'm through.

('Daddy').

These are mythic poems that transcend history, make it on their own terms.

In 'Tulips' Plath describes the larger-than-life flowers in a way reminiscent of Yeats' fearful description of the status 'Easter 1916' had assumed in the consciousness of the Irish nation. Yeats is one of Plath's influences, and was especially in her mind for the period that she was living on Fitzroy Road in London, where Yeats had once lived and where Plath wrote much of *Ariel*. Yeats had observed with perplexity and sorrow and awe that the individuality of the players in the drama of 1916 had become assimilated into the monolith of historical event:

Hearts with one purpose alone
Through summer and winter seem
Enchanted to a stone
To trouble the living stream.
...The stone's in the midst of all.

Plath's tulips are similar perhaps because they prophesy her subsuming of individual personality in an absolutist quest for purity: 'Now the air snags and eddies round them the way a river/ Snags and eddies round a sunken rust-red engine...' We as readers now snag and eddy round Plath.

Durcan has no such heroic aspirations. On the contrary, his instincts are anti-heroic. This is the reason Yeats is subverted in 'Geronimo', the poem where the judge and his son visit the Sligo lake district and tell the story of Pearse's visit to Corkery. The point of the story is Pearse's annoyance at the lapping of water that kept him awake all night, a swipe on Durcan's part at the nostalgia for the West that saturates 'The Lake Isle of Inisfree', where the poet is lulled not irritated by peace drop, drop, dropping and, like a slow torture, 'lake water lapping with low sounds by the shore.' 'Geronimo' can convincingly be read as a parodic reading of Yeats' much anthologised poem, a standard post-prandial recitation at bourgeois tables, Durcan's chosen battlefield.

Ariel made history by appearing to step out of it, while Durcan's poems, immersed in history, revise it and, therefore, make it in more modest terms. How many times do we see his father reading the *Irish Independent*? 'Daddy, Daddy' as a cultural historical record is very much about being a male in the generation after that which created Ireland's independence. Its revisions of history are coterminous with revisions of Irish identity, particularly male identity. Durcan strips away the layers of denial beneath the displacement that figures the nation as a woman, 'Mother Ireland', by honestly exposing the feminine in the individual male identity which resists the purity and polarity of stereotype. The title *Daddy, Daddy* underscores a moment in Irish history when a male writer identifies with a woman, one significantly who is not Irish and not bound up with issues of nationhood, the traditional turf of the Irish male writer. Durcan regularly makes forays into issues of social sensitivity in Ireland, especially those related to sex, like contraception and divorce. These politics are not a minor part of his poetic. In 'Daddy, Daddy', for example, the politics of the family is Durcan's ambit, a territory traditionally regarded as a female preserve. Durcan is identifying with Plath both as a fellow suffering human being and as a poet strategist. I take his unexploitative, brotherly embrace of Plath, a poet sibling from a similar family drama, as his way of expanding the margins of Irishness at the end of the century, softening and humanizing the harsh profile of the archetypal founding father.

Whereas Plath's father in 'Daddy' appears to be a statue of Thor toppled and sprawled in the sea, 'a head in the freakish Atlantic', Durcan's father is a loyal member of Fine Gael, upright, conservative, but recognizably human, a product of his times. When the poet fantasises about a statue of his father it will be made in wood, not stone, and fashioned by an unlikely sculptor, a butcher in Sligo whose shop, to be very exact, is on Wine Street. This unpretentious, born artist bears the prophetic surname, Quirk, not a bad appropriately imperfect rhyme with Durcan who has deliberately refused to be a denizen of Parnassus. He too has a specific address in the real world which makes his poetry parochial in the way Kavanagh urged, less intense than Plath's, but more grounded, resolutely human. Durcan, therefore, will avow in 'Ulysses' with both deference toward and difference from Plath: 'Daddy, Daddy,/ My little man, I adore you.' This could not be a more intertextually deft and complex line. It both once again echoes Plath with that key word 'adore' and deviates from her simultaneously. Durcan is adoring not a 'fascist' but 'my little man', someone from whom and for whom he has gained detachment and affection in equal and interdependent measure. It's a deliciously ambivalent remark, not possible in Plath's more extreme but also narrower emotional repertoire. Durcan finally manages to cut his father down to size and give him at the same time a sweet kiss on the cheek.

Paul Durcan and the North: Recollections

Edna Longley

'Meeting Paul Durcan on the top deck of a bus in Cork City' may sound like a preparation for parody, but that is how I first encountered him. During the hot summer of 1976 Michael Longley and I were spending a month in Cork where John and Evelyn Montague had lent us their house on Grattan Hill. This was a base from which to visit Hedli MacNeice at Kinsale. At that stage we had agreed to write the Louis MacNeice biography (a task later handed over to Jon Stallworthy). We did make a start on the enormous box of papers in Hedli's house but, as she had injured her leg, we spent a good deal of time looking after her granddaughter and her granddaughter's friend, taking them to the beach with our own children and Oonagh Montague. It was also a chance to get a better sense of Cork, a city associated with my father. But among all the plans and accidents of that visit, the meeting with Paul Durcan made the most lasting impression.

I recognised him at once. This says something about poetry and physiognomy — the latent iconicity that draws painters to poets' heads — since I had only seen him across a crowded bar in Inniskeen in 1974, the year he won the Patrick Kavanagh award, the year Michael was a judge. However, I had reviewed *O Westport in the Light of Asia Minor* for the *Irish Times*, rather grudgingly and snootily, I'm afraid. It was by getting to know Paul that I came to appreciate aesthetic premises that differed sharply from those of the Northern poets on whose work I cut my critical teeth. Whatever their own great differences, they all subscribed to the intense lyric or concentrated verbal pattern — not that object of political sneers, 'the well-made poem', but Keith Douglas's 'every word must work for its keep'. I do not imply that Paul Durcan's words are slack or idle, just that their conditions of employment are framed in other terms: servants rather than constituents of a vision. He writes prolifically, at times journalistically, as if compelled to mediate all existential pains through poetry. Intensity comes into play at the fault-line between Durcan's imagination and the world (producing his generically strange blend of fantasy, prophecy and satire), not when a poem crystallizes. Durcan is fully a Romantic in that Poetry takes precedence over poems. This way of working also resembles D H Lawrence's preference for 'the poetry of the present moment' as against the poetry of the beginning and the end, its cold perfection. But, as with Lawrence, abundance means that you sometimes get a double intensity. 'Birth of a Coachman', astutely picked by Brendan Kennelly for the *Penguin Book of Irish Verse*, is such a poem. Its sheer pace activates a small cosmos as the life-cycle and Irish landscapes are swept into the projected hectic journey of 'the man of the moment/ Who is now but a small body of but some fleeting seconds old'.

Nonetheless, a continuing rage for order led me to think about the desirability of a Durcan selected poems. This proposal, first to Paul himself, then to Blackstaff Press, also responded to his slightly chaotic publishing history, marked by a tendency to move on. Ultimately he moved on from Blackstaff, too, but I think the *Selected Paul Durcan* (1982) provided a bridgehead from which the first phase of his achievement could be appreciated and new readers won. Selecting the poems was itself a revelation. He came to

Belfast with his lists, I made my own suggestions, then we argued to the point of exhaustion. His attachment to poems often depended on their mystique within a value-system whose terms were not strictly aesthetic. This is true of most poets, but with different nuances. For instance, the elegies for Micheál Mac Liammóir and Cearbhall Ó Dálaigh were non-negotiable. It was not only publishing with Blackstaff that introduced Durcan's poetry to the North. From the first reading he gave in Belfast, and he has now given many, he acquired a cult following here too. In the rest of this essay I will suggest that the Northern literary links that Paul Durcan developed in the late 1970s have a symbolic as well as a practical meaning. To look at the North in his poetry, or to read his poetry from the North, is to highlight a crucial context.

The meeting on the bus naturally produced a meeting in a pub (Henchy's in St Luke's). What moved Michael and me as Paul talked was how passionately he cared about the violence in Northern Ireland. That this should come as a surprise might show either that we had become remote from life in the Republic, or that life in the Republic had become remote from what concerned us. In fact, Durcan's poetry presses on distances and exclusions of that kind: 'The Protestant graveyard was a forbidden place', 'The native who is an exile in his native land', 'National Day of Mourning for Twelve Protestants', 'Don't suppose Derrylin will ever be prestigious as Auschwitz:/ "So what?"' As a citizen of the Republic, who had been working in the North since October 1963, I obscurely felt repatriated, welcomed home, by the attitudes expressed in Paul's conversation and manifested in his work. Any later engagement I may have had with North/ South cultural politics probably goes back to 'meeting Paul Durcan on the top deck of a bus in Cork City'. But the mutually sealed-off frontier between North and South in 1976 was, obviously, a more than personal barrier, and it extended into intellectual as well as social life. While writers and academics who no longer lived in the North — the White Russians as some wag called them — were (on the whole) sympathetically received in Dublin, and proceeded to make friends and influence people (the journal *Crane Bag* was in the womb of time), internal Northern literary affairs remained curiously shrouded from view. This may have been a fertile rather than a claustrophobic circumstance. It enabled younger poets, such as Paul Muldoon, to develop in their own way, and stay sensitive to their environment, without being subject to certain kinds of publicity and interrogation. The spotlight turned on the Northern scene was patchier than legend maintains. And, of course, channels of communication could be opened up if you tried. Writers like Thomas McCarthy, Neil Jordan and John McGahern, followed in the 1980s by Nuala Ní Dhomhnaill and John Banville, also shattered any notional iron curtain when they came to read in Belfast. Cross-border literary traffic was one of the small preparations for Glasnost. Nonetheless, Paul Durcan's interest in the North mattered (and matters) because it was paradigmatic. He not only crossed the border: he dramatised the problems of border-crossing.

Durcan's response to Northern Ireland is conditioned by, and beamed at, the Republic. Its co-ordinates and dynamics are quite different from those of, say, Seamus Heaney's poetry. Accordingly, he has raised some Northern hackles (besides risking hate-mail and worse), as when he impartially scorns all paramilitaries. 'In Memory: The Miami Showband: Massacred 31 July 1975' approaches this loyalist atrocity by quoting 'a patriotic (sic) versifier' who 'whines into my face: "You must take one side/ Or the other, or you're but a fucking romantic"'. Some readers of the poem object to an obvious Provo-supporter being satirically targeted in such a context. But that — as with 'In Memory of Those Murdered in the Dublin Massacre, May 1974', which ends by implicating those who would commit similar murders for 'a free Ireland' — seems to be the point. With a particular eye on Irish nationalism, on his own crowd, Durcan manipulates and exposes the reflexes of selective sympathy. In the titles of these poems his seemingly over-rhetorical insistence on 'massacre', a word historically attached to sectarian slaughter (Milton's 'On the Late Massacre in Piedmont'), is counterpointed by academic precision as regards dates. This tension between exactitude and what looks like exaggeration signals the strategy of Durcan's pacifist poetics. He presents violence as the outcome of monstrous fantasies that sacrilegiously deny the minutiae on which life and creativity depend: 'You made music, and that was all: You were realists/ And beautiful were your feet'. Art is realist; 'fucking romantics' kill.

Yet Durcan's pacifism is (interestingly) complicated by his familial ties to John MacBride and Maud Gonne MacBride. 'The Minibus Massacre: The Eve of the Epiphany' laments that:

...the graves of the 1916 leaders
Have all been dug up
By Irish-speaking Chicago-style gangsters
With names like Ó Brádaigh, Ó Connaill;
And Pearse's skull used as a hurling ball
On O'Connell Street Bridge;
And John MacBride's shin-bones
Used to make hurling sticks
With which to whip-lash Pearse's skull
Up and down the bridge ...

This, like many utterances from the Republic during the 1970s, distinguishes between the violence of the 1916 leaders and that of the latterday IRA who are also seen as foreign, spuriously 'Irish'. The dishonoured relics of Pearse and MacBride (compare 'MacDonagh's bony thumb') value a spiritual inheritance which must have force if it can be abused. Durcan's sense of outrage here partly stems from his feeling that a family shrine has been violated. (His family's historical investment in the state continued to influence even the anarchistic extremes of his aesthetic.) Similarly, 'Margaret Thatcher Joins IRA' (February 1978) morally equates the Provos and the Tories while setting Wolfe Tone, 'a thoroughgoing dissenter', apart from both groups in his hallowed grave.

In the 1980s, however, such distinctions disappear as a tactic or perspective. And there is no longer any implied contrast between the errors of his father's generation and a more heroic political past, with which the poet identifies as he scourges contemporary violence. Durcan's elegies now stick to the present, often using voices or devices which underline the incongruity between particular deaths and society's official values. Thus in 'The Murder of Harry Keyes' Catholic bishops do not issue 'statements/ Of 'widespread condemnation' and 'wholesale denunciation', but go on 'an underwear strike/ Outside the offices of the IRA in Londonderry and Belfast'. They then say 'Howdee' to those who come in or out. The second voice in the Derrylin poem,'The Feast of St Bridget, Friday the First of February 1985' (another elegy whose title ironically invokes the religious calendar) alternates between '*So what?*' and '*Maybe so*' while the first voice simply reports the shooting of a bus-driver in front of schoolchildren. In 'Poem Not Beginning with a Line By Pindar' Durcan returns to the minibus

massacre more than a decade later. For the 1916 references in
the earlier poem, he substitutes a 'judgement' by 'Daddy...The
President of the Circuit Court/ Of the Republic of Ireland'
who says: 'Teach the Protestants a lesson'. Obviously it is the
poet who has become the truer 'judge', taking agonised
responsibility for the complicities and ambiguities of Irish
nationalism, handing down advice as to how it might be
redefined. In a sense this is Dublin claiming a poetic authority
which its politicians have evaded. Durcan's commentary on
the North, with its stress on unadmitted Catholic sectarianism,
intertwines church and state in a corrupting mutual hypocrisy.
His own acts of conscience or contrition have absorbed
Yeats's exclamation: 'What if the Church and the State/ Are
the mob that howls at the door!' Such poems make Northern
violence central to Durcan's critique of the Republic and
make the Republic central to Northern violence. It is the
Republic that provokes methods that are more politically
direct than those employed by any Northern poet caught in
the local tangles (a comparison with Michael Longley's
minibus massacre poem, 'The Linen Workers', might be
instructive). Thus 'The Dublin-Belfast Railway Line' begins:
'What I want is free rail travel/ For the heroic democrats of
the IRA'. Perhaps 'At the Grave of O'Donovan Rossa, 1989',
a far cry from Pearse's oration, encapsulates Durcan's
progress towards radical revisionism:

Not Irish merely but English as well;
Not English merely but Irish as well.

Durcan's horror of violence may make some of his
methods *too* direct. They invite the kind of antithetical
backlash that typefies and stultifies public discourse in the
Republic (see, for instance, Declan Kiberd's suppression of
his political poetry in the *Field Day Anthology*). But grief
about the North also finds more oblique outlets. It is

profoundly internalised in another couplet-poem 'Ireland 1972', here made familial in the psychic terms of a Freudian family romance: 'Next to the fresh grave of my beloved grandmother/ The grave of my first love murdered by my brother'. 'The Night They Murdered Boyle Somerville' (also from *O Westport*) powerfully understates its means of situating the Northern conflict within a longer history. It builds up slowly from the speaker sitting in an empty railway carriage travelling 'south through the west'. 'A small old woman with her husband who was smaller' enters the carriage and starts to talk. The poem might be read as an Irish variant on Philip Larkin's 'The Whitsun Weddings', but passes through 'the fields in their summer' with darker matters on its mind than that symbolic 'condition of England' journey:

> *Nor did we evade each other's eyes*
> *Nor pronounce solutions to the awful war-in-progress*
> *Except by a sign-language acknowledging*
> *That here was the scar that lay inside the wound,*
> *The self-betrayal beyond all chat.*

The old couple (like other old people in Durcan) transcendentally evoke an ancient past that merges into a utopian future: 'He was a king-figure from out the islands of time'. Time and rules are suspended when a ticket inspector fails to enforce the prohibition '*Ná Caith Tobac*' and withdraws 'apologetically, apologising for the intrusion'. The repetition of apology reinforces a kind of homage to this king with his 'ritual blowing of an ancient pipe'. But history intrudes again into the timeless lull as the woman speaks 'of the old times and the *scoraíocht*/ Back in Skibbereen and of the new times and the new words'. Her husband utters the understatement that lies *inside* the poem's understatement, and the historical scar bleeds:

'Ah but,' he interposed, glaring out into the
  blue-walled sky
'I found out what was in it and what was not in it,
The night they murdered Boyle Somerville;
I knew then that it was only the sky had a roof.'

The single, factually shocking line which gives the poem its title refers to this Anglo-Irish admiral's murder by the IRA in west Cork in 1936. It capitalises on the local and literary resonances of his surname.

'The Riding School' (published in *Crazy about Women*, 1991) is a more recent exercise in oblique angles. It turns an Irish poet, a representative rider of Yeats's winged horse, into a humble groom:

Dung, cobble, wall, cypress;
Delight in art whose end is peace;
No cold-eyed horseman of the Irish skies
Can compare with me
Leading out the Grey of the Blues

Durcan plaits various refrains into this mantra, divided between plain text and a refrain-stanza in italics with no main verb and internal repetitions: *'The blindness of history in my eyes/ The blindness of history in my hands'*. The speaker's pacific refusal to impose opinions ('I talk to my song;/ My song talks to me') implies the demands that any aesthetic opposed to violence must make upon itself. Anger erupts only when the peace-poet confesses his weariness: 'My song is nearing the end of its tether;/ Lament in art whose end is war;/ Opera glasses, helicopters, TV crews;/ Our slayings are what's news'. Here, as in all his best political poems, Durcan lays out his own sensibility to be savaged by history.

'The end of art is peace' continues a long trail from Coventry Patmore to Yeats to Heaney. In his fine poem 'The Harvest Bow' Heaney offers the poem itself as a peace-offering: '*The end of art is peace*/ Could be the motto of this frail device...' Yet the 'foetal and penitential' inclinations in *Field Work* (1979) are inevitably crossed by other urgings from the 'invisible, untoppled omphalos' of the Northern Catholic community. Durcan has written two poems which engage in playful dialogue with Heaney, and which are well aware that, if the poets converge on certain propositions, they set out from different points of the Irish and artistic compass. The first, 'Seamus Heaney's Fiftieth Birthday', may have acquired fresh relevance as a reflection on the interplay between a poet, his public and publicity:

> *I am disconcerted by all this cant of your fiftieth*
> * birthday,*
> *Yet here I am at the sill with my tray of images,*
> *Finding as I had hoped and half-expected*
> *A 'Please Do Not Disturb' sign on the door knob.*

Durcan draws on the vocabulary of Catholic ritual that he shares with Heaney to assert the primacy of the poet's inner sanctum: 'Do they not yet know the stations of innocence?' Then he cites Heaney's poem 'Sunlight', in which his aunt baking scones becomes emblematic of 'love': 'You who, without cant, in our time/ Redeemed the noun 'oven' from the rubric of murder/ And gave back to us a verb of our mother.../ That one day we would feel warm enough to speak'. This tribute is more cunning than it seems. Durcan 'misreads' Heaney in the direction of his own brand of pacifism and his own historical obsessions. 'A Spin in the Rain with Seamus Heaney' (significantly set in the Northern limbo of Donegal) contrasts the poets' literary strategies in the idiom of table tennis: 'Myself standing back and leaping about,/ Yourself standing close and hardly moving'. Durcan notes, however: 'What chiefly preoccupies us both is spin'. This poem, too, may have a spin on it. Durcan's affectionate banter with Heaney makes room for difference, as for similarity, but he knows that they compete for laureateship in that sphere where Nationalist Ireland talks to itself and debates whether to let other people in on the conversation. The game of ping-pong is no accidental metaphor. 'A Spin in the Rain' once again ends on Durcan's terms. Its winning shot asserts a common definition of poetry as a spirit that, with a blend of courage and technique, challenges violence:

Poetry! To be able to look a bullet in the eye,
With a whiff of the bat to return it spinning to drop
Down scarcely over the lapped net; to stand still; to
*   stop.*

Paul Durcan's poems are among the texts I have taught in a course called 'Irish Poetry After Yeats'. His impact on a Northern university classroom must surely differ from his impact on a similar group in the South. When we discuss poems written by 'Ulster poets', I try to establish an intertextual sense of their aesthetic, cultural and political dialectics. This elicits the complex critique working through poems (and which students themselves can bring to bear), and it guards against the perspective of one poet or poem predominating. No student should feel either alienated or too cosy. When we come to Durcan, however, his work functions as a liberating relief from local hang-ups. This is not only because he introduces 'revisionism' to Protestants, or lively lampoons of the Church to Catholics, but because his language and images tell them that the international youth culture of the 1960s is also part of Irish literary history. Without necessarily liking everything he does, they learn that you can be serious about Ireland without being po-faced. And

when I play a tape of Durcan reading 'The Riding School',
nobody says anything for a minute afterwards.

Spin

Ruth Padel

1

'A Spin in the Rain with Seamus Heaney' is Durcan playing, and playing at being, Heaney. The two are out together for a drive; and a sudden knock-up at ping-pong. Game and journey — both are images of poetic strategy.

I note that we are both of us
No mean strikers of the ball and that, although
we have different ways of addressing the table —

Myself standing back and leaping about,
Yourself standing close and scarcely moving —
What chiefly preoccupies us both is spin.

'Spin' starts the poem by referring to the journey. It ends, through Heaneyesque alchemy of the concrete image, by referring to the ball. The 'spin' shared is double: drive, or movement through a poem; and ballplay, wordplay. Heaney's car holds both poets, and circles round on the way like Durcan's poem which also holds them both.

Heaney's game-technique is 'standing close and scarcely moving'. Driving, though, he 'circles upwards' in:

...an upwards-peering posture
Treating the road as part of the sky,
A method which motoring correspondents call
Horizontal-to-the-vertical.

He gets out of a traffic jam:

With a jack-knife U-turn on a hairpin bend
With all the bashful panache of a cattle farmer —

A typically tender Durcan appreciation of personal style.
Heaney's thought through a poem is non-divertible (on and
up, horizontal to vertical), but his language can zip back on
meaning and avoid word-clog. Durcan's spin works
differently. He presents himself as passenger; here, teasingly,
a passenger taking formal, Heaney-like control ("Look — I
can do it too") of spin through a poem. The torsion of Durcan's
poem comes through his affectionate images of Heaney's
style, Heaney's spin.

When not playing Heaney, Durcan moves otherwise
through journey and game. 'Standing back'. 'Leaping about'.
He has anyway characterised himself as a wilfully passive
non-driver:

I am forty-five and do not
Know how to drive a car...

Forty-five years of sitting in the back seat giving
    directions...
Forty-five years of not caring to know the meaning of
    words
Like transmission, clutch, choke, battery, leads...

('Self-Portrait, Nude with Steering Wheel')

His technique is backseat: to seem to let words take charge.
'Not caring to know' the meaning of some words, standing
back from them, is the dead opposite of Heaney's dive into
the resonances of names for things handled and used. The
Durcan posture seems to let words drive him. His spin is of
course as controlled as Heaney's ('no mean strikers of the

ball'), but is radio-control, the art of a snake-charmer, not the hands-on approach of a potter.

2

Movement through his poems (spin as forward drive) comes from three other sorts of spin, I think. First the ball-play: the apparently inadvertent rolls-over of meaning words perform in his neighbourhood; the to-and-fro current set up between their different meanings. Then from the human version of this: an alternating current of sympathy or identity spinning between two people. Finally, from the spin of the poem's thought: which moves forward in backstitch, going over the same ground newly, advancing by repetition and coil.

In 'Doris Fashions', forward movement comes from wordspin on the words of the title. From one line to the next they turn suddenly, Escher-like, from adjective and noun to proper noun and verb. The poem's persona is passive observer on parole, waiting for 'the prison van' to 'collect' (as if 'Paul Durcan' could be collected) 'me'. Avoiding his self-image in the window, he re-thinks the words on it:

I caught a glimpse of myself in the display window
Of a shop across the street — Doris Fashions.
I glimpsed a strange man whom I do not know...

I averted my eyes from the mirror-image in Doris
    Fashions,
Yet thinking that it is good that Doris Fashions —
That there is that much
To be salvaged from the wreckage of the moment —
That Doris Fashions.

The two words roll over on their tummy for him, like a pet. Like a pet, they become as he strokes them a route into warmth, the warmth of other ways of being, away from bleakness and parole:

If you had a daughter called Doris, and after you had
*   spent years*
Rearing her and schooling her and enjoying her and
*   loving her,*
She left home and set up shop in a country town
And called it Doris Fashions — how would you feel?
You would be proud of her, wouldn't you?
Or if you fell in love with a girl called Doris
And it turned out she had a little shop of her own
Called Doris Fashions — you'd be tickled pink,
*   wouldn't you?*

The new verb is an old-fashioned word for what an artist or god does. The shop-name rustles suddenly with creation, daughters, lovers. Durcan turns wordspin into the drive of thought and feeling which propels the poem and the imprisoned persona away ('Doris Fashions Paul Durcan — Paul Durcan Doris Fashions') like the tail of a rocket, to explode in affirmation. No prison van, just 'the road out to the prison'. Words, the world's messages, fashion 'a road out'. The poet is acted on by them as if he'd stepped fresh into a safari park of little saviours.

For who made the world?
Doris made the world —

Adam naming in Eden comes surrealistically to mind.

The human correlative to this is the back-forth coil of identity between two figures. The poet's persona flows into the other person, seeing 'I' through 'your' eyes. In so many poems to 'you', 'I' gets lost in ('and I very nearly drowned'

— 'Nessa'), hurt by ('Don't Daddy, don't, Daddy, don't, Daddy, don't' — 'Study of a Figure in a Landscape 1952'), comically and inappropriately overcome by desire for, 'you':

> *Why you, Michelle? why you?*
> *Will you join me? Join me?*
> *If you're the joining kind, please join me...*

> ('The Beckett at the Gate')

The roll-over of identity happens with lovers, fathers, friends, daughters — and strangers. What is it in these lines from 'The Hat Factory' (1976) that shouts 'Durcan'?

> *Probably, I shall never wear a hat:*
> *So thus I ask the old man*
> *If I may look at his trilby —*

Is it what Brendan Kennelly called his 'manic confidentiality', coming at you here in the first line? Or the tonal register, lunging into the school-essay formality of 'thus', with its biblical undertow? Tentativeness: 'Probably' followed by a comma? The pacing of 'I'? The word comes on the same stress in the line for three lines but moves back a syllable each time: underlining the disingenuous self-scrutinizing ('I shall never' in relation to 'wearing', and all 'wearing' implies). Or the polite subjunctive, 'if I may'?

Well — all this: but more than issues of voice, tone, register and pace, it is the emotional move, out into the other person. 'If I may look at' turns into handling (and handling entails, as with Heaney and Doris, thinking about creating, focus of the poem's title). Durcan moves from 'looking' to touching and entering the object; the procedure of his later painting poems. 'At his trilby' marries formality to a polite involved tenderness which couldn't quite come from anyone else except maybe Beckett, in *Watt*. The world is suddenly full of Giacometti-ish lone men, holding objects which decisively

interest others. 'Lovely irises you have — let me touch them',
as the bus conductor says in 'Our Father':

I apologized to him as I dismounted at Dartry.
"Sorry, but I have to get out at this stop."
"Don't be sorry — be nice to your irises.'

As the bus swerved away from the kerb, I thought:
Amn't I the lucky breadman that I got the Dartry bus...

Shift and spin of being, between two figures, gets caught
up in the all-pervading spin on words. Part of 'your' impact
on 'me', is that 'I' solitarily perceives fuller meanings in
'your' words: as in the satirical 'What Shall I Wear, Darling,
to *The Great Hunger*?'

'I' receives these word-symbols from other people
desperately, gratefully, crossly, ruefully, in delight or
irritation:

I was fed up with people barking at me,
"Have you not seen Barry McGovern's Beckett?
Have you not been to the Beckett at the Gate?"
There's a Beckett at the Gate, there's a Beckett
    at the Gate

Spin between 'I' and 'you' mirrors the spin of meanings
among words, and also the coil of thought through a poem.
Poems seem blown about, back and forth, by seemingly
random associations and repetitions, spiralling back on
themselves in circular progression. At the end of 'Our Father',
after the bus conductor and reminders of a father who always
wanted his son to get this bus, not Number 13:

I press the bell to Mummy's apartment...
I stare up into the surveillance camera lens...
...I know she can perceive
The panic in the pupils of her son's eyes...

She says that she does not understand my new book of
poems
Which are poems I have composed for my dead father.
"But" — she smiles knowingly — "I like your irises."

Circling back with those flowers, Durcan spins on their name.
Being liked for your irises is being liked for your own panicky
interrogation centre ('I am a suspect in an interrogation
centre'), the centre from which 'I' see 'you', and reflect 'you'
in 'me'. Iris as flower becomes iris as the dot of the eye —
or 'I'.

Motoring correspondents who know Greek might call this
method of self-propulsion *boustrophedon* ('ox-turn' — from
ploughing), name for the earliest Greek form of inscription.
Instead of starting each line fresh on the left, the archaic
stone-cutter folded his second line back from right to left,
under the first. There were no gaps between words anyway:
you went on carving letters back along the underneath line so
what you had to say became a sort of a tapeworm squashed
down over the stone. 'Doris Fashions Paul Durcan / Paul
Durcan Doris Fashions'.

Durcan's *boustrophedon* backtrack is his version of
Heaney's 'U-turn on a hairpin': not U-turn so much as
continuation back and under. Words get picked up and
expanded on the next line:

A source disappearing,
Source of all I am before my eyes disappearing.

('Glocca Morra')

The Mass-like repeats refine, enlarge, and carry forward:

The early morning sunlight carries in the whole street
from outside;
The whole wide street from outside through the

> *plate-glass windows;*
> *Wholly, sparklingly, surgingly, carried in from outside.*

       ('In Memory of Those Murdered in the Dublin Massacre,
                         May 1974')

The position in the line of the repeated words here is *boustrophedon* in itself. 'From outside', at the end of the first line; on the inside of the second; and back to the outside edge at the end of the third.

In 'Raymond of the Rooftops', the poem moves towards revealing the full awfulness of the man's words:

> *I asked my husband if he would*
> *Help me put back the roof:*
> *But no — he was too busy at his work*
> *Writing for a women's magazine in London*
> *An Irish fairytale called Raymond of the Rooftops.*
> *Will you have a heart, woman — he bellowed —*
> *Can't you see I am up to my eyes and ears in work,*
> *Breaking my neck to finish Raymond of the Rooftops,*
> *Fighting against time to finish Raymond of the*
> *   Rooftops,*
> *Putting everything I have got into Raymond of the*
> *   Rooftops?*
> *Isn't it well for him? Everything he has got!*

Their awfulness comes over new by repetition in a different context:

> *There was I up to my fat, raw knees in rainwater*
> *Worrying him about the hole in our roof*
> *While he was up to his neck in Raymond of the*
> *   Rooftops.*

By spiralling on words, thought, personal identity, Durcan gets a voice, and a line, that seems to think aloud: that seems to get everything in. What's in the mind, as well as what's out there. The only poet at the moment with anything like Durcan's control in this region has also developed a unique style: C K Williams, artist of the long line. In his innovation, his way into getting everything in, line comes first: as if voice came through the stretching of line. With Durcan, you feel persona and voice came first, and line happened by accident.

With words, people, and thought, movement in Durcan's poems comes from persona, plus the illusion that this persona is passively acted upon by world and word. Another person's logo becomes his:

All my life I've dreamed of having a motto of my own...
Waiting for the prison van to collect me,
In the window of Doris Fashions I see into myself
And I adopt as my own logo, my own signature tune,
Doris Fashions —

('Doris Fashions')

He 'averts his eyes' from his own reflected face:

Hurted, hurtful,
All that ice, and all that eyebrow.

Instead of his own reflection, he takes the world's autonomous messages, which whirl him through and out of the poem. Persona is the prime material. World's effect on it causes the spin.

3

The way this persona is moved, is moved about by what's other and outside, moved wholly into another identity, makes Durcan unique among male poets at voicing women. He must have worked long on this. "You buy ice-cream cones," he tells Heaney in 'A Spin in the Rain'. "I buy women's magazines".

Spin

How many *Women's Owns*, with their confidential offering-up of intimate details, of sharing precise solitary ways of doing physical things, especially to appearance and body, have gone into this voice?

> *At closing time he kissed me on both cheeks*
> *And we bade one another goodbye and then —*
> *Just as I had all but given up hope —*
> *He kissed me full on the mouth,*
> *My mouth wet with alizarin lipstick*
> *(A tube of Guerlain 4 which I've had for twelve years).*
>
> ('The Haulier's Wife Meets Jesus on the Road
> Near Moone')

Heaney, in his 'Personal Helicon', says 'I rhyme/ to see myself,/ to set the darkness echoing'. To Durcan, self-image comes back not from darkness and wells but voice and women. Self-image appears in Doris's window; self's logo in her words. His women's voices present a mercury-backed view of the male self in its (apparently) true, scuffed, rueful, hopeless, colours:

> *I will admit it is difficult for a man of forty*
> *Who has spent all his life reclining in his wife's lap...*
> *A man cannot be a messiah for ever,*
> *Messiahing about in his wife's lap...*
> *Painful as it was for me, I put you down off my knee*
> *And I showed you the door...*
> *So that the sunlight shone all the more squarely*
> *Upon the pure, original brokenness of our marriage...*
>
> ('The Pietà's Over')

The writer's wife in 'Raymond', the Haulier's Wife (on the road near Moone — or the moon), Phyllis Goldberg ('Thank you for making love to me. Love. Phyllis Goldberg'), the woman driver sexually ignored by a hitch-hiker with a moonstone rosary ("I was that — that mystified" — 'The Soldier'): all are disappointed by men but gamely turn their attention to other things and in doing so highlight their own generosity alongside male hopelessness:

> *That night, thinking about him in bed,*
> *I realized that he was a soldier*
> *Come back from, or going to, the wars.*
> *A gentleman with no hope — no hope at all.*
>
> ('The Soldier')

Most women in Durcan are disappointed — except the nun:

> *I was an old nun — an agèd beadswoman —*
> *But I was no daw.*
> *I knew what a weird bird I was, I knew that when we*
> *Went to bed we were as eerie an aviary as you'd wish*
>   *to find*
> *In all the blown-off rooftops of the city...*
>
> ('Six Nuns Die in Convent Inferno')

This is Durcan's 'Wreck of the Deutschland' but its joy in the nun's friskiness of thought could never have come from Hopkins:

> *God have mercy on our whirring souls —*
> *Wild women were we all —*
> *And on the misfortunate, poor fire-brigade men*
> *Whose task it will be to shovel up our ashes and shovel*
> *What is left of us into black plastic refuse sacks.*
> *Fire-brigade men are the salt of the earth.*

The poet identifies with his nun's 'exotic loneliness':

> *Never to know the love of a man or a woman;*
> *Never to have children of our own...*
> *All for why and for what?*
> *To follow a young man — would you believe it —*

Who lived two thousand years ago in Palestine
And who died a common criminal strung up on a tree.

That 'Palestinian' makes one man, one embrace, which does not disappoint women. This elderly nun is delighted bride:

...Christ is the ocean
Forever rising and falling on the world's shore.
Now tonight in the convent Christ is the fire in whose
*   waves*
We are doomed but delighted to drown.

His persona's apparent passivity, the way it gets moved by things and words, lets Durcan eel over into an alien country. *Going Home to Russia* added to the other-country metaphors (Mahon's Delft, Longley's Troy, Heaney's North, Tóibín's South) for Irelands:

...he is speaking to an Irish dissident
Who knows that in Ireland scarcely anybody is free
To work or to have a home or to read or write.

If a woman's voice is a backhand way of seeing self from the other side of the veil, a foreign country, the other side of an iron curtain, is a great way of writing about home:

It is not until I am aboard the carrier
That I realize that I am going home...
                    ('Going Home to Russia')

Contact with the foreign (especially being lifted by a 'carrier') is sex, and landing in Russia is making love:

In the aftermath of touchdown, gently we taxi:
We do not immediately put on our clothes.

While making actual love in Russia is 'coming' home:

Closer to you than I am to myself.
My dear loved one, let me lick your nose...
Isn't it good, Svetka, good, that I have come home?

A foreign woman is two kinds of foreignness at once: perfect for describing self as the foreigner who (as in 'The Pietà's Over') needs to be guided and swaddled:

And Svetka said in Russian: "These foreigners
They cannot even keep from falling out of bed —
Always needing to be treated like babies."
The wagon-lady grunted and slid the door shut
And I climbed back into the bunk with Svetka.

('The Red Arrow')

Self-revelation comes through foreign voice:

Stalin Street was deserted
As we embraced goodbye.
She remarked:
'I like you a little because you have mixed feelings.'
...Galya,
Can there be anyone in the world who has not got mixed
    feelings?
Should there be anyone in the world who has not got
    mixed feelings?

('The Woman with the Keys to Stalin's House')

4

Despite the women's voices, poetry's spin (both journey and game) comes over in Durcan as a specifically male thing: see under Heaney and the 'ice-cream cones' he buys. (No poem so far features a knock-up with, for example, Eavan Boland.) Above all, a fathering thing. Fathers are synonymous with drive:

> *Leaving behind us the alien, foreign city of Dublin,*
> *My father drove through the night in an old Ford*
>   *Anglia,*
> *His five-year-old son in the seat beside him.*
>   ('Going Home to Mayo, Winter, 1949')

And with games: 'There were not many fields/ In which you had hopes for me...' so he says to his father in 'Sport'. 'But sport was one of them'.

It is as if male pain — effort, balls, never doing well enough — hurt the persona into poetry, and especially into poetry's search for strangeness, as the way of going home. Put 'Going Home to Mayo' from 'alien' Dublin, against 'Hymn to My Father':

> *Yet you made me what I am —*
> *A man in quest of his Russia...*
> *O Russian Knight at the Crossroads!*
>
> *If you were me — which you are —*
> *You would go home to Russia this very night.*
>   ('Hymn to My Father')

But also hurt him into poetry as deadly game, the never-finished battle for, and of, technique:

How many thousands of times, old man,
Did you strike a high ball for your young son
To crouch, to dart, to leap,
To pluck the ball one-handed out of the climbing air?

('The One-Armed Crucifixion')

All this underlines the ending of 'Spin in the Rain':

Poetry! To be able to look a bullet in the eye,
With a whiff of the bat to return it spinning to drop
Down scarcely over the lapped net; to stand still; to
*   stop.*

Like the poem's form, this is homage to another sort of father: Durcan playing (in both senses) Heaney. It belongs to Durcan's picture both of Heaney's style (described as exactly this, 'scarcely moving', 'standing still') and of the content Heaney takes on (looking bullets in eyes). But it answers also to Durcan's sense of a father-coloured, sportive male 'will':

It was my knowing
That you were standing on the sideline
That gave me the necessary motivation —
That will to die
That is as essential to sportsmen as to artists.

('Sport')

The lethal seriousness of male 'play', the desperate image of self apparent (at least to female eyes) in such play, speaks to testosterone even in the ping-pong of poetry. It is fathers who care about ballplay:

I may not have been mesmeric
But I had not been mediocre.
In your eyes I had achieved something at last.
On my twenty-first birthday I had played on a winning

team
The Grangegorman Mental Hospital team.
                    ('Sport')

So the Durcan image of poetry, inevitably perhaps, is male journey, male game — except occasionally, when there's a special woman ('Woman Footballer of the Year'), or a specialist sport that does not involve balls, not directly:

I said: Nuala —
You are a born knucklebone player.
She whistled: I am —
I am a born knucklebone player.
          ('The Knucklebone Player')

But fathers have daughters too. Daughters come into father-poems as the redeeming note. They help to merge self into father: as in the wonderful somersault of identity in 'Glocca Morra', father's death-bed written as a letter to daughter. At dad's death, the word 'dad' spins — to mean not father but poet:

Dear Daughter — Watching my father die,
As one day you will watch me die,
In the public ward of a centre-city hospital...
Dear Daughter — When the time comes
For you to watch me die,
In a public place to watch me
Trickling away from you...
... check out the music in the next bed.
"How are Things in Glocca Morra?"
Every bit as bad as you might think they are —
Or as good. Or not so bad. Love, Dad.

5

What does all this say for self-manifestation as snail?

I spin out my fate
Under my lady's capstone...
Round and round I trundle my bundle of ego...
The Great Irish Snail in his prime...
I am not a womanizer,
I am a snail.

('A Snail in My Prime')

'Snails' are all through the newest collection (as the idea of 'going home to Russia' was, in that collection), not just in the last poem. They begin operations in the poem for Mary Robinson:

Old Man curled up...
Beats his wings,
Opens his overcoat, a grandfather clock
Adjusting his pendulum, tugs at his waistcoat...
Picks up his walking stick, stands vertical...
Begins to lift up off the snow at an angle
Of forty-five degrees. He ascends, tick-tock,
Past her bedroom window.

The little-girl-who-will-be-President sees this snail-clock tick-tocking past her window. He promises to hug her when she's President:

She swears to herself in her sleep...

I will live all the days of my life
Looking out of my window...

Keeping faith with the mountain:
The mountain as snail...

> ('Woman of the Mountain')

What resonances make 'snail' so important? Is it the sense of signature, the defining pattern of your very own shell?

...my extended family
In shells all of different stripes and hues
But unisoned in a bequeathal of slime.

But the Durcan image reverses your basic ideas about snails: the privacy into which persona retreats. Durcan uses vulnerability ('Eyes out on stalks') as a rapier. His poems are not interested in snail as self-protection. Instead, they care for 'slime' — that pre-Socratic vision from the end of 'A Snail in My Prime'. 'Primal' matter ('Older than the pyramids'): the glistening, fertile, random, persistent, generous sludge or glue binding human relationships and poems.

So slime is at the bottom of it: combined with journey and spin. All that slow inching forward: poem as long organic journey (no clutches, leads, or batteries), humping a spiralled persona, an outward-looking face, on its back.

A spiral shape — a circle that goes somewhere new — is created by geometric tension, go forward, retreat, go forward. As Durcan's poetry moves:

Death is a revealing of light
When a snail inherits the sky,
Inherits his own wavy lines;
When a snail comes full circle
Into the completion of his partial self.

The winged snail from 'Woman of the Mountain', spinning along with limbs trailing passive but waving behind, his inmost spiral the face of a clock, his own face looking out straight at the reader, is on the cover of *A Snail in My Prime: New and Selected Poems*. It refers to the child's vision in that poem. But it seems to sum up Durcan's whole poetry's self-image. Part-man, part-shell, spinning to his own tick-tock.

Tea with Paul Durcan at Dusty's Café

Bruce Woodcock

Paul Durcan's work has been slow to catch on in England. It wasn't until the publication of *The Berlin Wall Café* in 1985 that he began to receive widespread attention. Yet by then he had already published six collections from 1967 onwards and had a *Selected Poems*, edited by Edna Longley and issued by Blackstaff Press, which won the Poetry Ireland winter choice in 1982.

Perhaps the slow English response is something to do with the infamous English reserve. Durcan's verse is too loose, extravagant and adventurous for established tastes. The English establishment still seems to prefer verse which stays within the bounds of a decent tea-cup - usually containing cold tea. Whereas Durcan's froths abundantly over the limits like an over-enthusiastic pint of Guinness. *Daddy, Daddy* is no slim volume: it's 185 pages and looks like a novel. After all, chaps, if we are to keep up poetic standards and keep winning the prizes, such breaches of decorum must be ignored.

Ireland, now — well, that's a different story. Always quick to hail good work when they see it, the Irish have been relishing Durcan for these last fifteen years or so. When I was in Dublin in 1990, which is where I picked up Durcan's *Daddy, Daddy*, in every bookshop and many another shop which just happened to carry a stock of books, along with the compulsory mountain of editions of Yeats, and the less predictable but very welcome pile of the complete Kavanagh, there was the unexpected sight of Durcan's new book regularly stocked in quantities it would be difficult to imagine finding in even a major Dillons or Waterstones.

Durcan's is poetry of the immediate present, to invoke D H Lawrence's formula. He has all the sparky expansiveness of Lawrence or Whitman, but without the ego. His work is necessarily hit-and-miss. He risks writing too much, and often utilises a seemingly loose baggy verse which has no limits. He has a capacity to apparently transcribe directly from experience, but then transforms the directness through a bizarre surrealism. As a result, his work can be hugely funny, an absolute refreshing delight for poetry-readers these days. Or he articulates apparently throwaway material into ornate, almost folk-ballad forms which have a strangely hypnotic quality. A sign for a clothes shop, 'Doris Fashions', repeated intricately through a poem, becomes a testimony to creative existence. The most unexpected and seemingly recalcitrant notions are shaped into forms which elevate them into a strange music, as in 'The Kilfenora Teaboy':

I'm the Kilfenora teaboy
And I'm not so very young.
But though the land is going to pieces
I will not take up the gun;
I am happy making tea,
I make lots of it when I can,
And when I can't — I just make do;
And I do a small bit of sheepfarming on the side.

Oh but it's the small bit of furze between two towns
Is what makes the Kilfenora teaboy really run.

By the time you hear that refrain for the fourth time, it has taken on all the peculiar musical magic of Coleridge's 'Kubla Khan'. This is all the more evident when Durcan reads his own work. A spare, lean-faced, serious-looking man, slightly built and unassuming, once he begins his readings he becomes oracular, mesmeric, a bardic presence: he sings, sways, chants, his hand drawn across his forehead and down across his face in apparent exhaustion, while he has his audience in stitches or agony, or both.

Durcan's work has an instantaneous quality, signalled in some of his newspaper headline titles: 'Archbishop of Kerry to Have Abortion', 'Margaret Thatcher Joins IRA'. He has peculiar fable-like poems, such as 'The Man Who Thought He Was Miss Havisham' or 'The Man with Five Penises'. Within this framework, he achieves a bizarre satirical effect. His targets are the Church, class, materialism, sexual stereotypes, masculinity. But for all these satirically absurdist elements, Durcan's work can etch a painfully personal, almost confessional pattern, as in the magnificent series of poems dealing with his marriage in Part 2 of *The Berlin Wall Café*.

Daddy, Daddy intensifies and extends Durcan's range and achievement. It is an explosively powerful book in seven sections. The first three on their own are a book's worth of poems akin to *The Berlin Wall Café* style. Poems recount incidents such as receiving a birthday greeting card from a daughter living in Canada:

It's one of those
Tall as telephone booth
Birthday Cards
With three words
In black capitals:
JESUS LOVES YOU.

Sweet and thoughtful of her.
Inside it continues in italics:
Everyone Else Thinks You're An Asshole.

'Self-Portrait, Nude with Steering Wheel' is a self-castigation by someone who can't drive:

45 years sitting in the passenger seat
With my gloved hands folded primly in my lap
— And you think I'm liberated.

45 years getting in and out of cars
And I do not know where the dipstick is
— And you tell me that I am a superb lover.

45 years of grovelling behind a windscreen
— And you talk of my pride and courage and
self-reliance.

45 years of not caring to know the meaning of words
Like transmission, clutch, choke, battery, leads
— And you say that I am articulate.

Durcan always gives the impression of catching experience in full flight, risking the snapshot immediacy of his language in order to create the feeling of being in direct touch with processes of thought, feeling, articulation. If there is a danger of verse-journalism in this, such cavils are readily abandoned in the face of the pay-off. And his delight in spinning yarns should warn us off seeing his kind of poem as somehow a transcription or life study. He is as much a fantasist as journalist.

This is made explicit in the long poem, 'Around the Light House', which comprises Section 4 of the book. It envisages the poem's speaker swimming beside a pregnant woman and her boyfriend in The Light House Cinema in Dublin. It is a dream sequence which concludes with the suggestion: 'In reality fiction is all that matters'.

As if to contradict that immediately, in Section 5 comes a ten-page semi-historical piece, 'Nights in the Gardens of Clare'. This is a verse dialogue between two lovers, one a local silversmith from County Clare, the other the daughter of a Spanish ship's captain, who survived the wreck of the Armada vessel *San Marcos* in September, 1588. Durcan has presumably taken this incident as a significant moment in the conflict between England and Gaelic Ireland, which was then undergoing the savage colonial terror of Elizabeth's deputies. It was a moment of potential armed resistance which foundered at Kinsale in 1601 when the Irish rebel Hugh O'Neill, Earl of Tyrone, was routed in battle, and Ireland made to submit to the bloody invasion. For the locals in the poem, though, the shipwreck of the Spanish is merely a spectacle, an entertaining disaster: 'It'll be surely great crack'. And that contemporary populism indicates the trans-historical nature of this dialogue. Despite the explicit date, it includes reference to Boethius Clancy (Clare's trendiest film maker), Shannon Airport, and the girl Soledad who dresses in skintight blue jeans. For this is a contemporary dream love-song whose plea is for a hopelessly optimistic vision of the future:

After the war is over, after we have all died
And have been born again, over and over, born
  again over and over,
There will be a time for loving and a time for smiling.

And that note of qualified hope is one which permeates other parts of this often agonising book, not least in the final two sections.

These contain poems focussed around a father figure, the 'Daddy' of the book's title. One of the remarkable elements of Durcan's work has always been his ability to address issues to do with being a man, male power, masculinity, and to do so with an emotional directness and honesty which is perhaps unexpected in male writing. In this set of poems Durcan approaches the relationship of father and son with a Plath-like intensity. Given the bizarre fictionality of Durcan's work, it is difficult to say where fiction ends and reality begins in such apparently naked confessional writing. To all intents and purposes, the speaker's father is Durcan's father, named as Judge Durcan in one poem, an ex-teacher who became the President of the Circuit Court of the Republic of Ireland, a media personality, a supporter of Fine Gael and Mussolini, 'voice of a harsh judiciary/ Whose secret headquarters were in the Home Counties or High Germany'. He is the generic equivalent of Plath's 'Daddy' from *Ariel*, the male fascist; except that here the victim is another male, a son who has to undergo ECT and periods as an inmate at various mental institutions to mediate the injuries inflicted on him by his father. And it is this contradiction which helps account for the agonising humour and tortured affection displayed in these poems.

Other writers have dealt with the father-son relationship with emotional intimacy, most notably Tony Harrison in his ongoing 'The School of Eloquence' sonnets. But Durcan's work makes Harrison's look what to some extent it always has seemed, problematically nostalgic. Durcan manages to twist anger, bitterness, love, sorrow and hard-headed analytical awareness to form a searing insight into the nature of masculinity and the effects of men on men. Durcan's 'Daddy' is 'saint and murderer', the wounded angel of the book's cover-painting, blindfolded, his swan's wings shot through, carried on two bare poles by his sons, 'two small brutes in hard hats'.

Except that the speaker of these poems is a son who has failed to make the grade as a man or brute, and was classified insane as a result. This allows Durcan to explore the devastating effects on men of their power without in any way wishing to abdicate from responsibility or make false claims for sympathy. Partly he achieves this through his bewildering blend of contradictory emotions into a bleak humour that is guaranteed to twist the knife for most male readers. One poem recounts how the speaker for once manages to play the role of successful male for his father's approval:

> *I may not have been mesmeric*
> *But I had not been mediocre.*
> *In your eyes I had achieved something at last.*
> *On my twenty-first birthday I had played on a winning*
>   *team*
> *The Grangegorman Mental Hospital team.*
> *Seldom if ever again in your eyes*
> *Was I to rise to these heights.*

But the situation is not one of simple antagonism or antithesis. Durcan also recognises the complicity between men. So there are poems in which at the age of six the speaker marries his father, getting divorced at twelve to marry him again when he's forty-four, just before his father dies. The pull and tug of male emotional bonding between father and son is seen at its most ambiguous in poems like 'The Two Little Boys at the Back of the Bus', father and son, sharing the same mother and the same game, rugby:

> *A parody of homosexual aggression:*
> *Scrum, hook, tackle, maul.*

We thought it right and fitting,
Manly and amusing,
That our clubs were named
After barbarian tribes.
You played for the Senior Vandals,
I played for the Junior Visigoths,
Our life's ambition was to play
For the Malawians
Against the Springboks
In Johannesburg,
Drinking lager,
Putting the boot in,
Taking the boot out ...

Isn't that what we've always yearned for,
Father and Son,
To be old, wise, male savages in our greatness
Put to sleep by Mother?

In their blank or sarcastic truth-telling, these poems get really near the bone of sentiment, embarrassment and sheer pain. But they are by no means hopeless in their attitude to the experiences they expose. Besides the humour, Durcan employs the ambiguous and shifting currents of affection, particularly in later parts of the section dealing with the son's response to the father's illness and death. And there is a built-in plea for change. This is explicit in the poem 'The Children of Lir' about Hugo Simberg's cover painting: 'Daddy, Daddy — O Wounded Angel — / When will you deploy your wings?/ When will you see that all your sons are brutes?'

It is this desire for change which presumably led Durcan to head the 'Daddy, Daddy' sequence with the single long poem 'Amnesty' which makes up Section 6. It is a poem about feeling imprisoned, about the prison of names and words which Daddy forced on the speaker as a small boy, words like 'Apartheid' which, we are told in another poem, Daddy pronounced 'With such élan, such expertise,/ With such familiarity, such finality,/ As if it were a part of nature,/ Part of ourselves.' But the poem in Section 6 is also about contradicting Daddy's law by courting a black girl from Cape Town. Durcan calls the poem after the name of their child which the speaker reiterates like a prayer:

And after we've made love
My wife puts me back down into sleep,
Oblivion,
By seashelling into my ear the lullaby of our daughter's
  name.
Amnesty
In the key of A minor
Into the seashell of my ear, the lullaby of my fate —
Amnesty

In this bitter love-war between father and son, amnesty in itself is a hopeful concept, and one which later poems in the sequence incorporate with painful affection.

Daddy, Daddy is an extraordinary collection; but then Durcan is an extraordinary poet. Not least because of his direct appeal as a communicator, he manages to cross the boundary between poetry readers and non-poetry readers with deceptive ease. An exiled Dubliner I know read Durcan and was so hooked by the immediacy of the voice and the local detail that she felt homesick and burst into tears. And then there was one of those peculiar coincidences that only seem to happen in Ireland. I was staying in Sligo after being in Dublin, and happened to go to a seaside place some miles away called Enniscrone. The front comprises sand-dunes backing a long beach, a car park with a children's playground, and a small amusement arcade full of appallingly noisy video games. And attached to the arcade is Dusty's Café. Dusty's is a bit like a 'transport caff' my dad used to take me in when I was a nipper years ago when he was on the lorries — "Jake's caef," he'd call it, assonating the two vowel sounds. You got the best bacon butty and mug of tea on the Great North Road. Anyway, I'd finished my mug of tea at Dusty's and went in to pay. The woman behind the counter took my money and then the following conversation ensued:

Woman: (presumably Dusty) That'll be Paul Durcan I see you're reading.

Me: (flabbergasted) Er, well, yes it is; it's his new one.

Woman: And you are enjoying it?

Me: (warming to a literary debate) Yes, do you know him? — (meaning his work)

Woman: Oh sure now — didn't he used to be always coming down here every year for his holidays when he was younger.

Me: (astounded): Did he?

Woman: He did; and many's the time he's been in here for some tea with his Da.

Me: (warming to potential research material): And have you seen him lately?

Woman: No, you know, not really; but his brother was here only last week. Sure when you see him again, tell him "hello" from me.

And with that, I left. Outside an image of a half-naked little Paul Durcan, brandishing bucket and spade, scampered across the sand dunes chased by his father, and disappeared.

So, just in case you ever read this, Mr Durcan, Dusty says "Hello".

A Half-Open Letter to Paul Durcan

Brian Lynch

Dear Paul,

This is a very peculiar undertaking, isn't it? I was out in the garden today picking elderberries — - and that in itself sounds like the beginning of a poem you might write — thinking about this and I suddenly realized that I felt like that character in one of Carson McCullers' novels who was brought into a room, told to close her eyes and wait; left there and thinking she was alone she 'pooted' (farted) and was mortified to hear laughter: the room had filled with people gathered for a surprise birthday party. In this case the birthday, if that's what it is, is yours and I'm just a guest, but the faint whiff of embarrassment is shared, or should be, among the contributors. Are we supposed to pretend you're not there? Can't be done. And knowing that you will be reading this, am I supposed to be telling you to your face that you're a great poet and a grand lad entirely? Can't be done either. Even thinking both things, as I do, it'd be false to express them in this way, as it were with my eyes shut.

So it's not been easy writing this piece, and I know you'll understand I wouldn't be doing it except for the money — and said yes before being told it was to be all for love, no less. Do you remember how much we liked the story about Patrick Kavanagh sitting one day in the Bailey surrounded by a gang of cronies? Everyone, including Kavanagh, was suicidally hung-over, weighed down by thoughts of Being and Nothingness. At last Kavanagh lifted his head and groaned: "There's nothing, there's nothing in the world... a good shower of fivers wouldn't cure". And here I am, doing I know not what, and for nowt.

Thinking this, I abandoned the elderberries, went into the house and dug out an old notebook from our time together in Barcelona in the winter of 1968. What a waste of paper! Scab pickings about myself and Matthew Arnold, of all people, and hardly anything about what was actually happening. There is, though, this: 'Thursday November 28. Today Paul came into my room in the morning and told me Nessa was pregnant. I've never seen anyone look so happy... He looked out the raining window and said: "It's like a Westport day." When he's happy he always remembers the West.'

And a few days later there's this: 'A day entirely wasted. No work done at all... As Paul said last night, we can't even consider ourselves to be writers, never mind what kind or how good we are. "My fault," he said, "is laziness. I haven't done anything yet — though I consider myself potentially to be a great writer." True of me also.' Well, well.

And yet, as I sniff those ancient egos, I remember that I also have somewhere in my papers a note you wrote me in Barcelona rejecting self-centredness in favour of 'the great Third Person that is in all of us'. That 'Third Person' inspired me then and still does.

So, in that spirit, let me address the invisible audience and see can I say anything about that 'you', the one you used to imagine being told by his father: Never Durcan my doorstep again!

When my daughter Clare was eleven, I took her to hear Durcan giving a reading in the Lambert Puppet Theatre in Monkstown. When I asked her afterwards what she thought of the performance she replied: "I understood him even when he was nonsensical, and sometimes he was nonsensical and didn't even understand it himself." Since I record in the same diary entry Clare saying that when she grew up she wanted to be an 'earologist' — a good definition of what a poetry critic should be — I regard her remark on the reading not only as high praise, but also as an accurate description of Durcan's work, pitched as it always is between apparent amazements, unpatented absurdities and impossible what-ifs.

Durcan is a funny man. But it's not always easy to know when, or even if, he intends to be droll. The first time I experienced this uncertainty occurred the first time we met. That meeting took place in Kirwan's pub in Leeson Street — it must have been the winter of 1963 when I was in my first term in UCD — and from a brief exchange I remember only one thing this pale, hawk-faced and intense youth said to me: "If you see a beautiful girl walking down the street, what do you think?" Slow as a flash, I answered: "I think: There's a beautiful girl walking down the street." He looked at me — piercingly or pityingly?

It was, in hindsight, a good Zen answer (like many another in the 60s, I was soon into Alan Watts' Blue Penguin version of Zen Buddhism). But Durcan wasn't then, and isn't now, interested in solutions. The question was only being asked because he didn't believe it could be answered, or at least that it couldn't be answered in every-day language.

But when we were becoming friends it was a time for mysterious questions. Paul was especially keen on the first sentence in Heidegger's *Introduction To Metaphysics*: 'Why are there essents rather than nothing?' (essents meaning 'things that are'). I don't think he was much influenced by the rest of the book — there's nothing Germanic in the way Durcan's mind works. The question was the whole thing, simply to ask it was the answer: it functioned as a talisman, as proper names did and still do in his work.

In another notebook, from 1965, I read this: 'I met Paul Durcan today, on his way to his psychiatrist and Grangegorman. "How do you stand it?" I asked him. "It's better than living at home," he said. His best bet would be to raise a loan of some money and get the first boat out of the country, otherwise he'll end up in the looney-bin for ever.'

Our friendship became close when he was incarcerated in St Pat's and I visited him there every day for weeks. What was the problem? I don't know, simple wildness I think. Mad or not — and you have to remember that at that time R D Laing, a Durcan hero, was adding to the anguish of schizophrenia a glamour of other- blame that didn't serve — he was treated with courses of electro-convulsive therapy. ECT was serious, especially for someone so orderly in his memory.

In 1967 we published jointly our first book: *Endsville*. The typically hippy title, which I jibbed at a little, was his. The money — I think it was £67 — was mine. The cover was a drawing by John Behan and the printer was a man called Chichester (known as Chi-Chi, he was related to the later Prime Minister of Northern Ireland, James Chichester-Clark) who ran the Museum Bookshop across the road from Dail Eireánn. The book was almost ready for publication when Michael Smith, who was just then starting the New Writers' Press, asked us to publish it under his imprint, which we did.

The publication was marked by a bizarre poetry reading held under the auspices of Project 65. It took place for some reason in an upstairs room of a building across the road from the Project gallery, which was then in Abbey Street. For the occasion I dressed in a Darby O'Gill swallow-tail coat and a bright orange Donald Davies blouse. Durcan wore an Arab djellaba and sun-glasses—he looked like Lawrence of Arabia played by Blessed Oliver Plunkett. Both of us were blind drunk, Paul so pickled that his reading terminated in total incoherence.

As it happened Eavan Boland was there to review the event for the *Irish Times*. Her piece, kindly I think now, said we were 'like children giggling in church'. Such irreverence, though, didn't do Paul any harm where it really mattered. In John Ryan's pub, The Bailey, a hundred yards, yet a million miles, from Trinity College where Eavan Boland and others were saying their prayers, Patrick Kavanagh, whom Durcan and I venerated as a god, was chortling over *Endsville*. He was, as I remember it, particularly taken with the couplet called 'A First Confession':

> *"Bless me, Father, for I have sinned:*
> *I have not read Jean Genet."*

On this basis he declared solemnly: "I've found my successor. I pass my mantle to Durcan."

In that year, or it may have been 1968, I managed, through my mother, who was a Fianna Fail TD in the same constituency as Vivion de Valera, the owner of the *Irish Press*, to get Paul a job as a sports sub in the paper. He walked out the first night. Because, if I remember correctly, someone said something derogatory about Cassius Clay. The champion was his champion and "Float like a butterfly, sting like a bee" was one of his magic mantras. Another was Barry Maguire's song 'The Eve of Destruction'. Paul was given to roaring out:

"You may leave here for four days in space,
But when you return it's the same old place:
The pounding of the drums, the pride and disgrace,
And you tell me, over and over again, my friend,
That you don't believe we're on the eve of destruction".

The 'friend' may not have believed, but Paul certainly did. Apocalypse was in his air.

Apocalypse wasn't in the air in Glasnevin though. In many ways Durcan and I are opposites in character. One of the opposites that I think attracted me to him was my being a Northsider. His Southside, legal, paternalistic, upperclass (to me) background was a burden to him. The fatherless Lynches' large and tattered Glasnevin house and our large and rackety family, ruled by an often-absent matriarch, didn't care a flying fornication for respectability, and Paul, I think, felt at home there, playing mad games of soccer in our utterly grassless back garden. (But though he liked Glasnevin, he didn't care for the Bots: the nearby National Botanic Gardens, the place I loved, and still love, most on earth: he called it 'a vegetable museum'.)

What I remember most from those too-drunken days was Paul's literally fantastic sense of humour and wonderful gifts as a mimic. I can still see myself and our great friend Serena Condon sitting in the Long Hall helpless with laughter as he, doing the fruity voice to a T, elaborated an increasingly surrealistic monologue by Micheál MacLiammóir, on whom he had just paid an unexpected visit. It wasn't so much the acting onstage as the effrontery and bravery of continuing to ham it up offstage in lipstick and obvious wig that attracted Durcan to MacLiammóir. Taking acting as seriously as Paul does accounts for the way he can unsettle even people who know him well — however serious he is, the actor is always pulling your leg. The lengths to which he goes to achieve his effects may be judged by a story an Englishwoman told me recently: she'd gone to hear Durcan give a reading in ultra-staid Bath and along with the rest of the audience had been overwhelmed by the power and eeriness of Paul's performance; needing, however, to go to the lavatory she tip-toed out of the auditorium, took a wrong turning and found herself backstage; there she discovered part of the reason for the eerie atmosphere: a tape-recorder was playing a cassette of lonely wind-sounds. For Durcan, reality is a *coup de théâtre*.

When Paul moved to London with Nessa O'Neill — he worked in the North Thames Gas Board and then as a star-guide in the Planetarium (is it any wonder comic juxtapositions play such a large part in his work?) — we collaborated on a cyclo-styled magazine called *The Tuppenny Book* in which I wrote, under the name Sailorson (there's a poem in *O Westport...* dedicated to him), a piece saying farewell to what I called 'handwriting poetry'. It signposted, I believe, the way Paul was already going: poetry meant to be spoken to as wide an audience as our hero, Bob Dylan, sang his songs. This was, I believe, the crucial decision in his writing life, but that option for democracy was, and remains, a unilateral declaration of independence — though he writes for the man in the street he continues to be a man in a cloud.

A 'stylist' of this kind can be evaluated by reference to E M Cioran:

> Inured to a purely verbal way of thinking, the sophists were the first to occupy themselves with a meditation upon words, their value, propriety, and function in the conduct of reasoning: the capital step towards the

discovery of style, conceived as a goal in itself, as an intrinsic end, was taken. It merely remained to transpose this verbal quest, to assign as its object: the harmony of the sentence, to substitute for the play of abstraction the play of expression...Having ceased to be nature, they (the sophist and the artist) live as a function of the word.

Cioran also says:

The artist...proceeds from the word to the actual: expression constitutes the only original experience of which he is capable...And since he aims at exhausting the capacity of words, he tends, more than to expression, to expressiveness. In the closed universe he inhabits, he escapes sterility only by that continuous renewal afforded by a game in which nuance acquires idolatrous dimensions and in which a verbal chemistry achieves compounds inconceivable to a naive art.

Durcan fits into this definition of the artist, but in his case his world is open to the world, the procession moves not from the word to the actual but the other way round, and, even more important, he is always trying to turn aside from expression as 'the only original experience'. Unlike a great many artists of our age, he has avoided disappearing into solipsisms and word-games.

But though the audience has received them, Durcan's best poems stand apart, being neither programmatic nor sectarian — what group could claim to be spoken for? Only the weak, the brave and the dead, especially those murdered by the bastard Provos, get a word in edge-ways.

It was in the autumn of 1968 that Paul, Nessa O'Neill and I took off for Barcelona. The poet Pearse Hutchinson, an old Barcelona hand, had supplied us with the names of two friends of his, Ernie Hughes and Soledad Pocaterra Thornton, and through them we hoped to get work teaching English. But hope was the only thing we'd planned in advance and jobs of any kind were not to be had, at least not immediately. Even though the cost of living was low, we were soon seriously short of money. Considering that a three-course meal with wine and brandy in our local restaurant, *La Panocha*, could be had for thirty-four pesetas (about twenty new pence), you can judge our poverty from the fact that there was a time when we were reduced to smuggling dinner, bread and tomatoes, into our pension for consumption on the premises. But the *Pension Alcoy*, situated down an unpaved laneway on the hill of Tibidabo, which overlooks the city, and run by Bongo, a Catalan who'd returned from Australia speaking a peculiarly macaronic English, was a suitably Durcanesque asylum for our austerities.

The wine, as I've said, was cheap. Cheapest of all, at about tuppence a litre, was *Vino Negro*, a highly alcoholic syrup so black that the morning after you'd think your teeth had rotted in the night. Paul thought he had a cure for the blinding hangovers it brought on: Coca-Cola. I remember one morning him rushing into La Panocha on the way to an interview for a job, ordering six bottles of the stuff and downing the lot in a matter of minutes. The cure was, it goes without saying, worse than the disease: the Coke came up on the underground, and the job fell down.

We weren't long in Barcelona when we were joined by Bill Bovell-Jones, an elegant and fastidious English photographer with a taste for Mr Fish shirts (very fashionable then) whom Paul had befriended in England. Bill didn't care for the asceticism of the *Pension Alcoy* — days were spent contriving to order an electric coffee-pot from Harrods (when it came, its plug wouldn't fit the socket) — but his acerbity was a thin skim over uncertainty and a sweet nature. Given the fact that we were living on top of each other, it's not surprising that we, as they say, fell out. I can still see Paul walking towards me at speed down an empty street and sweeping by without a word.

Almost ten years after that, in 1976 or 1977, I was living in Vavasour Square off Bath Avenue, and now, remarkably enough, considering the chaos of my papers, I lay my hand on a verse I wrote then. The piece is titled, prophetically, 'Beyond Argument':

Absolute silence.
I get the message.

Back from the pub
At lunchtime —
Eight gins in an hour —
Huddling in your coat
As I make up the fire.

"Poetry," you say,
"Is Jimmy Barry Murphy
With the ball on his stick
Racing through and slogging it
Into the back of the net.
Or Lester Piggott coming
Out of the starting gate."
(Riding Bustino at money on.)

"That," say I, "is not
A definition,
But a simile."

Eyes stare. Then close.
Head shakes:
"You're a desperate man
For the self-analysis."

Though that in fact
Was what you said
Later in the day,
Still it will serve.

An old friend
Is a cute whore.
Need I say more?

It was, I remember, a winter's day, very dark and gloomy. I hadn't drunk eight gins in an hour but I needed a pee. When I came back the front door was open and the Durc had disappeared.

But that isn't the point I end at, though it did mark an ending of sorts. Battered and all as both of us have been, not least by marriage, what I prefer to remember is opening that same front door on a day in July 1978 to see Nessa, the beautiful and daring woman who was my friend, with a long poem, an epithalamium, framed behind glass in her hands. The paper is now rather more than what *Private Eye* calls 'slightly foxed', but the handwriting, and the intention, is as clear as ever:

"Brian, it is almost
Noon, the flaming sun
In her flaming vestments,
    Gilt in her gold,
Like the years that like minutes
Speak, is inching her route,
Her gilt route to the matrix,
    Of her blue mould.

It is ten years since
You sped through the night
By train for Barcelona
    By a silent sea

153

Where, in a dried-up river
Bed, in the white dawn
Of your days, you searched
For that other "me"

Wanly without whom we
Pine, plod or perish
In an aching acre of alone-
Ness that is not right
For the brain or the body,
Mystics quickly admit it,
Delightedly, the need
For light in the night:

And for light in daylight
More so than in the night,
A supernatural flame
With a face in it:
A face in the flame,
Always to be remembered,
Never forgotten: the point
Of love's bayonet....

On the point of love's bayonet, much blunted from disuse, there's a purple stain that looks a lot like blood, but I prefer to say: Now, there's elderberries for you. Add yeast and there might yet be wine. Again.

As ever,

Brian
28 September 1995

Crazy About Women: Poems About Paintings

Brian Kennedy

Crazy About Women began on 27 June 1990 when I invited
Paul Durcan to lunch at Fitzers Restaurant in the National
Gallery of Ireland. I had never met Paul but I had been a reader
of his poetry and had been impressed by his highly visual
world of words and his frequent references to film and
painting. This had been highlighted for me in a fine article
written by Kathleen McCracken 'Canvas and Camera
Translated: Paul Durcan and the Visual Arts', published in
The Irish Review (Autumn 1989). The second strand of
thought prompting my luncheon invitation was an
appreciation of The Artist's Eye series of exhibitions began
in 1977 at the National Gallery, London, under the guidance
of Alistair Smith. I wondered if Paul might be interested in
exploring the idea of making an exhibition and a book of
poems inspired by his chosen paintings. We had an enjoyable
chat over lunch and I knew this passionate poet was interested
in the project when he told me that, daily for three weeks in
1980, he had visited R B Kitaj's Artist's Eye exhibition at the
National Gallery, London. We ended our first meeting with a
tour around the Gallery, talking about the pictures, European
Old Masters, Irish paintings and national portraits. From our
conversation it was evident that Paul had spent his life looking
at pictures, not just seeing them as some do, but really looking

at them. I was in enthusiastic mood, discussing pictures with someone who was equally unashamed to say he loved them and could not live without them. We parted as collaborators and as friends. When we meet today, even at irregular intervals, it is as though we had met yesterday and were taking up the conversation where we had left it the previous time.

A few days after our first meeting, I received a postcard from Paul saying that, if commissioned by the Gallery, he would give himself wholeheartedly to 'the book idea'. I discussed the situation with the Director of the Gallery, Raymond Keaveney, who supported the project fully and asked me to proceed to tie up the formal arrangements of contract and to work with Paul to develop an exhibition that would be a key element of the Gallery's programme for Dublin's Year as European Capital of Culture in 1991.

In early August 1990, just a month or so after we had first met, Paul visited the Gallery and we agreed on the key issues: that he would select the paintings for the exhibition, the manuscript would be delivered by the end of March 1991, and the exhibition would take place around November 1991. In early September 1990 Paul began, one might say, loitering with intent in the Gallery on a regular basis, becoming on first-name terms with the security attendants, scrutinising paintings on the walls of the display galleries, requesting to see paintings in the reserve collection, and seating himself, immersed in his thoughts and words, on a particular chair in the Gallery restaurant beside Albert Power's sculpture Fish.

I met with Paul on a number of occasions and, at his invitation, accompanied him around the Gallery to talk to him about the paintings. He was especially interested in how I felt about them, their effect on my emotions. We talked about many subjects of pertinent interest to art lovers: for example, the effect of light on pictures, the dislocated environment for art that we call a gallery, the way paintings change for us depending on our mood, the artistic tricks that painters use to lure us into their world of imagination, the vitality of visual culture, the necessity of training our eyes in the art of seeing and looking. We also discussed the cinema, literature, our shared interest in the work of Jack Butler Yeats, the conduct of arts policy in Ireland, travel to cities of the world, and events of the day (I remember particularly that Brian Keenan's release in August 1990 caused us to celebrate). We always sat to lunch in the Gallery restaurant at my favourite spot, beside Gustav Natorp's Knucklebone Player. The sculptures by both Power and Natorp were later to form part of the exhibition. I also received requests for information from Paul and their detail made me realize how seriously he was taking his curatorial responsibilities. He asked me, for instance, how would one describe the type of moulded foot at the base of the plinth in Hamilton's portrait of the Bishop of Derry with his granddaughter; what type of firescreen was used in Hussey's delightful interior with members of a family; who was Louis Cohen who gifted to the Gallery two splendid portraits by Jervas of Lady Mary Wortley Montagu. One day Paul asked to spend some time alone 'in silent contemplation' in my office where, at that time, because the French rooms were closed during refurbishment, Meissonier's masterpiece, A Group of Cavalry in the Snow, was hanging. Between September 1990 and the end of February 1991, the only other indication I had about the paintings in which Paul was especially interested was when he inquired about the availability of pictures that were in relatively poor condition, or about which works were scheduled to travel to loan exhibitions abroad. I was certain, however, that Paul was giving this project more concentration than any he had previously attempted because it was something that was hugely important to his art.

I received the near final list of paintings on 8 March 1991 and it was a delight, a personal selection combining well-known paintings by major artists and fine paintings by lesser-known artists. Paul had clearly ruminated on the travesty of justice that can be found in art history wherein some artists become famous, most with due reason, but others never achieve the renown their output deserves. I still did not know what the book and the exhibition would be called. Neither, I think, did Paul, and we agreed that the title was somewhere in his book and he would find it.

When the manuscript arrived at the Gallery a few weeks later, it was full of surprises, beginning with its title *Crazy About Women*. The National Gallery of Ireland had never been audacious or provocative in its promotional ventures, and the prospect of publicising and marketing an exhibition and accompanying book titled *Crazy About Women* was one we had never considered. Yet I thought then, and even more so now, that *Crazy About Women* marked a watershed in Paul Durcan's career as a poet. The book celebrates a time of *joie de vivre* when he was bathing in the exuberance of a world of pictures. His book was for me about love, maternal love, fraternal love, making love, looking for love, finding love, losing love, honouring the act of love-making. Suddenly the National Gallery of Ireland had to face the situation that it was about to engage in a project that challenged its public on non-artistic issues. Paul's poems, set as they are in the contemporary world, despite their references in *Crazy About Women* to paintings made over the last five centuries, described vividly the act of love-making, referred to homosexual love, to AIDS, to the fondness of some men for little girls, and also to making love in the grass, sharing a bath with a lover, jumping into bed in the middle of the day. This would be no ordinary National Gallery exhibition and accompanying publication.

Paul Durcan was concerned that the forty-eight paintings in Crazy About Women should be in strict chronological order and that the subject titles favoured by art historians should be used. He proposed that the magnificent and sensitive portrait of Giambattista Moroni, Man With Two Daughters, would make an ideal book cover and exhibition poster. The painting was an inspired choice as it was not well-known to the public but striking in its direct engagement with the viewer. There were autobiographical resonances for the poet, who has two daughters and who has been separated from their mother for many years. The multi-layering of the book's title became more and more apparent.

During the summer, Michael Breen of the design company Creative Inputs, Robert South of the printers Nicholson and Bass, and the photographer John Kellett, combined their skills to produce a splendid publication and the book arrived in the National Gallery on 27 September 1991. The Gallery's Curator of Exhibitions, Fionnuala Croke, organised a much admired hang of the collection of paintings chosen by Paul Durcan for the exhibition, Crazy About Women. I selected short extracts from each poem and these were displayed beside each painting to allow the visiting public to explore the marriage of poetry and painting wrought by Paul Durcan. On opening night, 15 October 1991, Paul gave the first of three major readings held in the Shaw Room of the Gallery, which was packed to capacity and the atmosphere electric.

Over the next few weeks Crazy About Women became a phenomenon. On 17 October The Gay Byrne Radio Show was transmitted from the National Gallery's temporary exhibition room. The acoustics of the room were superb, as Paul Durcan read poems from *Crazy About Women*. I gave brief introductions to the poems by describing the paintings as well as I could for the radio listeners, and Joe Duffy conducted some entertaining interviews with members of the Gallery staff. The highlight of the radio programme was a brilliant bluesy introduction on saxophone by one of the security attendant staff, Denis O'Loughlin, now sadly deceased, to Paul's rendition of the poem 'The Riding School', the refrain, or chorus of which, reads:

I in my red blanket
Under the Cave Hill Mountain
Leading out the Grey of the Blues:
The blindness of history in my eyes;
The blindness of history in my hands.

The poems and the exhibition were also featured on many other radio and television programmes in Ireland and England. President Mary Robinson made a private visit to the National Gallery to be shown around the exhibition by Paul Durcan. The Taoiseach, Charles Haughey, wrote to say that he was delighted by Paul Durcan's latest work, which was 'very beautifully produced and a treasure to have'. *Crazy About Women* was one of the best-selling books in Ireland, and on 2 November 1991 the National Gallery of Ireland had the distinction, perhaps unique for such an institution anywhere, of holding the number-one position in the best-seller lists. The book remained at number two or three in the lists throughout December. By Christmas 1991 some 20,000 copies of *Crazy About Women* had been sold. Over

40,000 people visited the exhibition at the Gallery between 16 October and 20 December 1991.

The Gallery's marketing campaign worked effectively, to the point that Crazy About Women came to be decoded by the public at large as the title of the Paul Durcan exhibition and book. Amusingly, the publicity we arranged with the Automobile Association was a little too successful. We received a call from the A A, informing us that the road signs distributed throughout Dublin advertising Crazy About Women were being stolen, probably by macho men who considered the signs ideal adornments for their bedrooms. The A A suggested that we add the word 'Exhibition' to the signs to make them less attractive to thieves.

The success of *Crazy About Women* was recognised by Macmillan Publishers who, in association with National Gallery Publications, London, commissioned Paul Durcan to produce a book of poems inspired by paintings in the National Gallery, London. This book, *Give Me Your Hand*, while being by no means a replication of *Crazy About Women* in its poetic content, was a direct compliment to the Irish-published volume, in that it was exactly the same size, with the same book cover format, typeface and design layout. On 5 May 1994 I visited the so-called Board Room of the National Gallery, London, the room where in 1980 Paul Durcan had spent days contemplating R B Kitaj's selection for the Artist's Eye exhibition. Fourteen works from London's unrivalled Old Master collection were displayed there, and I read with great enjoyment the poems of Paul Durcan which had been inspired by them. As I left the Gallery and walked out onto Trafalgar Square, I revelled in the journey that had begun over lunch some four years previously. Certain lines from *Crazy About Women* still live with me, conjured up by incidents in daily life. Some of the paintings in the National Gallery of Ireland will always be viewed with Paul Durcan's words singing in my ears. There are many truths in the lines of *Crazy About Women*, but one touches me particularly: *Art is private relations — not public relations.*

Orpheus Ascending
The Poetry of Paul Durcan

Derek Mahon

I'll start with a new Durcan poem, hitherto unpublished. It's called 'Poet Arrested for Distributing Daffodils in Castlebar':

I was sitting in Bewley's Oriental Café in Castlebar
On Easter Monday, oh such an Easter Monday
With the clouds chasing each other over the tables,
When my friend Michael Hartnett walked in
With a bunch of daffodils, the most shameless
Yellow daffodils you could ever imagine,
And distributed them with oriental courtesy
To the patrons seated with their Java and Earl Grey:
One for the dentist's wife, one for the dentist,
One for the priest's wife, one for the priest
And two for the Protestant girl from Killala
Who won the All-Ireland Junior Golfing Championship
*   in 1979.*

As my friend Michael distributed the daffodils
He murmured very gently, 'Pax vobiscum';
But before he had quite finished
There was a blowing of whistles and a crackle of
*   walkie-talkies*
and a flying column of the Garda Síochána came
*   rushing in*

Shouting, 'You can't do that here, you can't distribute
 daffodils
In Bewley's Oriental Café in Castlebar!
Where do you think you are? Granada? Belgrade?'
And they bundled him outside into the spring sunshine,
A last daffodil trailing from one hand.
Next morning District Justice Joseph Galtieri
 O'Higgins,
The man with the finest Toyota in Co. Mayo,
Sentenced the poet to six months' hard labour
Talking sense into the Provisional IRA;
And as he left the court between two Ban Gardaí
My friend Michael glanced over
And winked at me, saying: 'Beannacht Dé ar an obair'.

Now, as you've already guessed, Durcan didn't write this poem. I did; but it's not bad, is it? My purpose in reproducing it here is to demonstrate, if such demonstration were necessary, that there is such a thing as a recognisable 'Durcan poem'. This is a compliment. Only an original and memorable voice lends itself to pastiche: it's the mediocre who are inimitable. But the 'Durcan poem' has been in danger of growing predictable; or so I feared until now.

I recently re-read the 'Grand Inquisitor' chapter of *The Brothers Karamazov*, in which Ivan tells Alyosha his 'poem' about Christ's reincarnation in seventeenth-century Spain. Christ, you remember, appears during a particularly spectacular *auto da fé*, performs small miracles, and is promptly hauled off to the slammer. There he is visited after dark by the Grand Inquisitor, a local Torquemada, who asks him not to rock the boat. Don't undo our modification of your original doctrine, says the Grand Inquisitor, or I'll have you burnt as a heretic — to which Christ offers only a silent kiss in reply. Accepting this as a promise that no boats will be rocked, the Grand Inquisitor has Christ released, and the Son of God disappears into 'the dark streets and lanes of the city'. Shaw, in the preface to *Androcles*, writes of the disparate natures of Christ and Barabbas, and concludes that the crowd will always choose Barabbas. Ivan, the genial cynic, is a Barabbas; Alyosha, the holy fool, strives to imitate Christ. Ivan, like Barabbas, has the soul of a bourgeois; Alyosha, like Christ, that of an artist.

I approach the work of Paul Durcan in this altitudinous fashion because it is on such a level that it can best be understood. Certainly you can read him as a pop poet, as a satirist, as a verse journalist taking on the bishops and bombers; but there is more to him than that. We know what he is against; but what is he for? Well — not to put too fine a point on it — he is for the same things as Mangan in his *Autobiography*: 'all that is true and good and beautiful in the universe'. He is Alyosha as opposed to Dmitri or Ivan: a seeker and, in Rimbaud's sense, a seer. His is the poetry of a new kind of man, whence his appeal to feminists: 'Women and poets', said Graves, 'are natural allies'. If he reads strangely to us, it's because we haven't got there yet — or rather, because we never can. He doesn't write out of a future where we have yet to arrive, for that would be merely to anticipate. He writes from lateral imaginative zones which contain, as it were incidentally, glimpses of the 'dim coming times'. (I read *Ark of North* in this light, for example). But it's the laterality, the sideways look (not, despite his degree in archaeology and mediaeval history, the 'backward look'), the simultaneous presence of alternative modes of perception, that characterises his vision.

This may be the moment to dispel once and for all the widespread belief that he is a Surrealist, a belief based on misconceptions both of Durcan and Surrealism. The notion derives, I think, from his professed admiration for David Gascoyne, and from a two-line poem, 'La Terre des Hommes', in his first collection, *O Westport in the Light of Asia Minor* (1975):

> *Fancy meeting you here in the desert:*
> *Hallo Clockface.*

'La Terre des Hommes', though striking and memorable, is untypical of Durcan, being entirely visual and free of editorialising. I used to think of it as a Dali or a Magritte; now I think of it as a Durcan. The word Surrealism is used too loosely in any case. Duchamp's classic definition, 'the chance meeting of an umbrella and a sewing machine on an operating table', proposes something less amenable to paraphrase than Durcan's epigram — besides, Durcan is on record as disliking Surrealism, in which he detects, correctly, a streak of sadism.

As for Gascoyne, I think Durcan has been misunderstood. It was only the very young Gascoyne who was a Surrealist: with *Hölderlin's Madness* (1938) he abandoned the doctrine; and if we are looking for his influence, I think it's to be found where most of Gascoyne's best work is to be found, in *Poems 1938-42*, first published by Tambimuttu's Poetry London Editions, with illustrations by Graham Sutherland, and included in the *Collected Poems* under the heading 'Time and Place' — poems of mystical attention like 'A Wartime Dawn' and 'The Gravel-Pit Field', neither in the least Surrealistic, both in the English Romantic-existential tradition which goes back to Coleridge and Keats. No, Durcan is not a Surrealist but a Cubist, one transfixed by the simultaneousness of disparate experience, all sides of the question, the newspaper headline, the lemon and the guitar — a man with eyes in the back of his head. The poems are often obscure, but need only be held up to the light.

Francis Stuart, in *The High Consistory*, suggests that 'the artist at his most ambitious does not seek to change maps but, minutely and over generations, the expression on some of the faces of men and women'. Edna Longley, in her introduction to *The Selected Paul Durcan*, reads a poem like 'Irish Hierarchy Bans Colour Photography' as an attack on 'black-and-white attitudes'. I have compared him with Alyosha Karamazov, described by Dostoevsky as 'greatly agitated' by the Church's successful modification of Christian doctrine. Julien Benda, in *La Trahison des Clercs*, a book which needs to be re-read in every generation, remarks that the 'clerk' who is praised by the laymen is a traitor to his office. It's in the light of such observations that Durcan's political position may be estimated: in *Jumping the Train Tracks with Angela* (1983), 'Bogside Girl Becomes Taoiseach', the implication being that it's only a matter of time. This isn't Surrealism but real sexual politics, a natural consequence of 'Ireland 1972', which says it all:

Next to the fresh grave of my beloved grandmother
The grave of my first love murdered by my brother.

The cover of *The Berlin Wall Café* shows a dead blackbird by Edward McGuire, and I'm reminded of the early 'Lament for a Fallen Blackbird' with which I once heard Durcan mesmerise a late-night audience at a poetry festival in Amsterdam. The role of 'exemplary sufferer', in Susan Sontag's phrase, is one which he has courted, consciously or otherwise, throughout his career, as if obscurely aware that he is temperamentally suited to the role of sacrificial victim — Adonis, Actaeon and Orpheus in one. Durcan was married for many years to Nessa O'Neill and is the father of two daughters; and Nessa has been celebrated by Durcan *passim* since *Westport*. 'She Transforms the Ruins into a Winter Palace', 'She Mends an Ancient Wireless', and so on. Some of these poems are very fine. Now the Durcans are separated, and *The Berlin Wall Café* is, in large measure, a 'Hymn to a Broken Marriage'. To speculate about the reasons for the break-up would be impertinent, except in so far as Durcan has himself commented publicly on the background to this new collection. Speaking to Charles Hunter in the *Irish Times* in 1986 he said, 'I will rue for the rest of my life the fact that I put my work before my family... Poetry is an incredibly isolated activity... Heaven is other people: a house where there are no women and children is a very empty house.'

Durcan appears, if anything, more of a feminist than ever. (Perhaps 'womanist' would be better). Jesus, he tells us, was 'a lovely man, entirely sensitive to a woman's world'; he meets 'a KGB lassie' in the Moscow subway; there is some gender-bending reminiscent of that camp triumph 'Micháel Mac Liammóir'; and even the nuns in 'High-Speed Car-Wash' twirl gleaming parasols in the sunlight while they discuss the new Peugeot. One critic has remarked that this new collection 'elevates self-pity to a condition of heroic intensity'. I would go further and say that the heroism *transcends* self-pity. This is a heroic book, by a hero of the imagination — not only because, from despair, he achieves poems like 'The Jewish Bride' and 'The Pietà's Over', but because his womanism, which casts Nessa also in a heroic role (as he has always done), suggests mythical precedents. When he promises 'to woo her only and always in the eternity of my loss' and asks us to join him in praising 'famous women', it is as if mankind itself were on its knees in apology and supplication; and I think, for example, of the story of Orpheus and Eurydice.

Durcan, with a microphone for a lute, can, like Orpheus, charm the birds from the trees; he is that kind of poet. Eurydice, you remember, died of a snake-bite and Orpheus followed her to the underworld, where he persuaded Pluto to let him have her back. Permission was granted on condition that, before reaching the light, *Orpheus should not look back*. He did, of course, and Eurydice was lost forever; after which he turned gay and was killed by Maenads. Durcan has not, to my knowledge, turned gay, and he is in no danger from the Maenads. It's that backward look that interests me, as figuring — what? Despair? Doubt? Disbelief? The wife in 'The Pietà's Over' tells her husband,

> *It is time for you to get down off my knees*
> *And learn to walk on your own two feet,*

and later compares the cold light of day with the Resurrection:

> *I did not take the easy way out and yield to you.*
> *Instead I took the door down off its hinges*
> *So that the sunlight shone all the more squarely*
> *Upon the pure, original brokenness of our marriage.*

But where Durcan sees an empty tomb I see Orpheus ascending into the light, an exemplary sufferer, a hero of art, to resolve his despair in song, inspired by a lost Muse. He himself, and through him our perception of the world, are changed by the experience in just such a direction as Stuart indicates in my quotation from *The High Consistory*. 'Man lives *poetically* on this earth,' said Heidegger, a philosopher favoured by Durcan; and it follows that our poetry is a kind of politics, a politics of the soul. René Char called poetry '*la vie future à l'intérieur de l'homme requalifié*', 'the future interior life of requalified man'; and it's as 'requalified man' that Durcan has something new and important to tell us. This new collection is of a piece, in this respect, with his previous work, differing from it only in the intensity of its heroism, the renunciation of a sometimes too facile fluency for the taut strings of perfect artistry. Emerging into the light, he has given us his best book yet.

Notes on Contributors

Colm Tóibín's books include two novels, *The South* and *The Heather Blazing*, as well as *The Sign of the Cross: Travels in Catholic Europe*.

Fintan O'Toole is a columnist with the *Irish Times*. He has published two collections of essays, *A Mass for Jesse James* and *Black Hole, Green Card*; a study of Shakespeare's tragedies *No More Heroes*; and a book on the politics of the Irish beef industry, *Meanwhile Back at the Ranch*.

Eamon Grennan has published four collections of poetry. He recently received fellowships from the National Endowment for the Arts and the Guggenheim Foundation. He teaches at Vassar College and divides his time between the US and the West of Ireland.

Peggy O'Brien is an American who lived in Ireland for nearly twenty years, for much of that time teaching in the English Department at Trinity College, Dublin. She now teaches in the United States at the University of Massachusetts in Amherst.

Edna Longley is Professor of English at Queen's University in Belfast. She is the author of several works of criticism, including *Poetry in the Wars* and *The Living Stream*. She edited *The Selected Paul Durcan* for Blackstaff Press.

171

Ruth Padel's collections of poetry include *Summer Snow* and *Fusewire*. She has also written two works of non-fiction, *In and Out of the Mind* and *Whom Gods Destroy*.

Brian Lynch's debut with Paul Durcan in *Endsville* in 1968 has been followed by several collections of poetry, including *Voices from the Nettle-Way* and translations with Peter Jankowsky of Paul Celan's *65 Poems*.

Bruce Woodcock is a Lecturer in English at the University of Hull. His books include *Male Mythologies: John Fowles and Masculinity*, and a recently completed study of the Australian novelist Peter Carey for Manchester University Press.

Brian Kennedy is Assistant Director of the National Gallery of Ireland. His publications include *Dreams and Responsibilities: The State and the Arts in Independent Ireland*; *Irish Painting*, and *Ireland: Art into History* (with Raymond Gillespie).

Derek Mahon is one of Ireland's most distinguished poets. His books include *Selected Poems* and *The Hudson Letter*.

Acknowledgments

Acknowledgment is made to the editors of *Magill* where part of Colm Tóibín's essay appeared, to *Bête Noir*, where Bruce Woodcock's essay appeared, to *The Irish Review*, where Derek Mahon's essay appeared, and to Dermot Bolger whose idea this book was.